HOOVER INSTITUTION

SHULTZ-STEPHENSON TASK FORCE ON
Energy Policy

Reinventing Nuclear Power

Keeping the Lights on at America's Nuclear Power Plants

Jeremy Carl and
David Fedor

Hoover Institution Press
Stanford University
Stanford, California
2017

www.hoover.org

Hoover Institution Press Publication No. 683

Hoover Institution at Leland Stanford Junior University,
Stanford, California 94305-6003

First printing 2017

23 22 21 20 19 18 17   7 6 5 4 3 2 1

Manufactured in the United States of America

The paper used in this publication meets the minimum Requirements of the American National Standard for Information Sciences—Permanence of Paper for Printed Library Materials, ANSI/NISO Z39.48-1992. ∞

Cataloging-in-Publication Data is available from the Library of Congress.

ISBN: 978-0-8179-2095-1 (pbk. : alk. paper)

ISBN: 978-0-8179-2096-8 (epub)

ISBN: 978-0-8179-2097-5 (mobi)

ISBN: 978-0-8179-2098-2 (PDF)

Table of Contents

Foreword   i
Acknowledgments   1
Overview   1

Introduction   9

Diagnosing the Situation Today   13

Policy and Regulatory Options   28
  - State Regulators—Compensating Nuclear Plant Benefits   28
  - State Regulators—Internalizing Other Costs   36
  - State Legislators—Compensating Nuclear Plant Benefits   38
  - State Legislators—Internalizing Other Costs   42
  - Regional Grid Operators   43
  - Federal Agencies   58
  - Congress   69

Improving Nuclear's Value   83
  - Owners & Operators   83

Conclusion   92

Appendix A: US Civilian Nuclear Power Reactors   101
Appendix B: Recent Nuclear Plant Closures   107
References   109
About the Authors   115
Index   117

Boxes
Recommendations for Policymakers   7
Nuclear Power, Washington Politics, and Climate Math   11
License Extensions   22
New Nuclear vs. Existing Nuclear   27
Production Tax Credits So Far   77
Looking Ahead to Policies for New Nuclear Technologies   80

Foreword

Nuclear power alone will not solve our energy problems. But we do not think they can be solved without it. This is the crux of our concerns and why we are offering this book. It describes the challenges nuclear power is facing today and what might be done about them.

One of us, between other jobs, built nuclear plants for a living; between other jobs, the other helped make them safer. In many respects, this is a personal topic for us both. But here are some facts:

We know that our country's dominance in civilian nuclear power has been a key part of America's ability to set norms and rules not just for power plants in less stable places around the world but also for the control of nuclear weapon proliferation. We know that it's an important technology-intensive export industry too: America invented the technology, and the United States today remains the world's largest nuclear power generator, with nearly a quarter of global plants (more if you count the hundred power reactors aboard our navy ships at sea). Domestically, we know that nuclear power gives us reliable electricity supply at scale, supplying one-fifth of all of our power production and that nearly two-thirds of our country's pollution and carbon-dioxide-free energy comes from these facilities.

There are known risks and real costs to nuclear too, of course, but on balance we believe that the benefits for the country come out well ahead. Historically, much of the national nuclear enterprise has rested on the backs of the US federal government (and military) as well as on the ratepayers of the electric utilities who own or operate these facilities. The question today is if—and how—those same players will be able to shoulder that responsibility in the future.

When we first started looking into the nuclear question as part of our energy work at the Hoover Institution a few years ago through the Shultz-Stephenson Task Force on Energy Policy, we had our eyes toward the future: What were the prospects and roadblocks for a new generation of small, modular nuclear reactors? How about the licensing framework for advanced, next-generation plant designs? Could a new entrepreneurial portfolio approach help break through the nuclear fusion barrier? We wanted to know what it would take to "reinvent nuclear power." Soon enough, though, it became clear that it would not be enough to reinvent the future of nuclear power; if we don't want to make the commitment to finance and run the mature and already-depreciated light water nuclear reactors of today effectively, we won't have the option to make that choice tomorrow.

Nothing in energy happens in isolation, so nuclear power should be viewed in its larger context. In fact, we are in a new energy position in America today.

First, security. New supplies of oil and gas have come online throughout the country. This not only has reduced our imports but also given us the flexibility in our production that makes price-fixing cartels such as OPEC weak.

Prices are falling too, not just in the well-known oil and gas sectors, the result again of American ingenuity and relentless commercialization efforts in fracking and horizontal drilling, but in new energy technologies as well. Research and development in areas such as wind and solar or electric vehicles are driving down those costs faster than the scientists expected, though there is still substantial room to go. We also have made huge strides since the 1970s Arab oil crises in the more efficient—or thoughtful—use of energy and are in a much better position energy-wise financially and competitively because of it.

Meanwhile there is the environment. The good news is that we've already made a lot of progress. As anyone who experienced Los Angeles smog in the 1960s and 1970s can attest, the Clean Air Act has been huge for the air we breathe. On carbon-dioxide emissions, the progress is mixed, but the influx of cheap natural gas, energy efficiency, and a growing menu of clean energy technologies suggest promise.

Our takeaway from all of this is that for perhaps the first time in modern history, we find ourselves with breathing room on the energy front. We are no longer simply struggling to keep the lights on or to keep from going broke while doing so. What will we then choose to do with that breathing room?

To put a finer point on it: America needs to ask itself if it's acceptable to lose its nuclear power capability by the midpoint of this century. If so, then, plant by plant, our current road may take us there. Some would be happy with that result. Those that would not should understand that changing course is likely to require deliberate actions.

What would we be giving up if we forgot nuclear power?

An environmentalist might note that we'd be losing a technology that does not pollute the air or water. Radioactivity is a cultural and emotional concern for many people, but nuclear power produces a relatively small amount of such waste—at a predictable rate, with known characteristics, and with $30 billion in disposal costs already paid for. Perhaps surprisingly, nuclear power production actually releases one hundred times less radiation into the surrounding environment than does coal power. Overall, with a long track record, the rate of human injury caused by nuclear power production is the lowest of any power generation technology, including renewable resources.

Jobs are increasingly discussed in energy, as they have long been in other business policy. Nuclear power plants each employ about six hundred people, about ten times more than an equivalent natural gas plant. Many nuclear workers are midcareer military veterans with few other outlets for their specialized skills—one US nuclear utility reported last year that a third of all new hires at nuclear facilities were veterans. Often intentionally located in rural areas, nuclear plants are major economic inputs to sixty small towns and cities across America. The nuclear power technology and manufacturing supply chain is a global export business for domestic businesses—not just for multinationals but also closely held nuclear-rated component suppliers, forgers, and contractors.

Someone concerned with security can appreciate that the fuel for nuclear power plants can be provided entirely from friendly suppliers, with low-price volatility, and long-term supplies stored on-site and not subject to weather disruptions. Existing nuclear power plants use mature technologies with a long experience of domestic expertise in operations, oversight, and regulation. More broadly, a well-functioning domestic civil nuclear "ecosystem" is intertwined with our space and military nuclear capabilities, such as the reactors that power our aircraft carriers and submarines.

Finally, we shouldn't discount that nuclear power plants are today being built at an unprecedented rate by developing countries in Asia and the Middle East, driven by power demands for their growing industries and increasingly wealthy populations. Those new plants are as likely to be built and supplied by international competitors as they are our own domestic businesses and their employees. The United States has so far held a dominant position in preserving global safety and proliferation norms owing to the strength of our domestic nuclear capabilities. Looking forward, new nuclear power technologies are available that could improve plants' performance and the affordability of the power they generate. But tomorrow's nuclear technologies directly depend on a continuation of today's nuclear workforce and know-how.

In today's American energy system, our biggest challenges are now human, not machine. Nuclear power illustrates this: While these generators have sat producing a steady stream of electrons, year by year, the country and markets have shifted around them. As long as we keep the gas pedal down on energy research and development—which is important for the long term—our country's fine universities and research labs will ensure that new technologies keep coming down the pipeline as fast as we can use them. Often what is holding us back now is a lack of strategy and the willingness to make the political and bureaucratic changes necessary to carry one out. Technology and markets are moving faster than governments.

Nuclear power operators after Chernobyl and Three Mile Island were famously described as being "hostages of each other." Any mistake made by one would reflect on all of the others. In many ways, this was an opportunity that became the basis for the American operators' effective program of industry self-regulation. Today that phrase may have a new meaning. In recent years, the country's energy industry has become unfortunately politicized, with many of the same sorts of identity-values-based appeals that have come to dominate our political campaigns.

Technologies or techniques are singled out for tribal attack or support, limited by a zero-sum mind-set. In truth, the energy system is not something that can be won. Instead, it's more like gardening: something that you have to keep working at and tending to. Fans of gas or nuclear, electric cars or oil exports, fracking or rooftop solar—in the end all are linked by common markets and governments. Each shot fired in anger ricochets through the system, sometimes with unexpected consequences. This is why, for example, we support a revenue-neutral carbon tax combined with a rollback of other technology-specific mandates, taxes, and subsidies that would go a long way toward leveling the playing field. Ultimately, a balanced and responsive approach that acknowledges the real trade-offs between affordability, reliability, social impacts, environmental performance, and global objectives is the best strategy for reaching—and maintaining over time—any one of those energy goals. Our energy system has more jobs than one.

So while we find ourselves with breathing room today, we know that the path ahead is filled with uncertainty. The unforeseen developments that have delivered us to this point today could once again carry us to an unexpected situation tomorrow. Renewable resource costs have fallen faster than expected—can that pace be maintained as systems pass from plug-and-play at the margins to unexplored territory on the widespread integration or even centrality of intermittent generation? Natural gas has seen a boon throughout the country—how comfortable are we in betting the future on its continued low-cost ubiquity? Coal has always been available alongside nuclear on the grid as a reliable baseload backstop—can we take for granted that it will survive a new regulatory environment through a series of technological miracles? Taking control of the grid through the large-scale storage of power would revolutionize our relationship with electricity and should be relentlessly pursued—but what if the battery technology can not deliver by the time we need it?

We are optimists about our country's energy future. We are also realists. This book is about the nuclear situation today. But it is a mistake to compare the known challenges of the present with the pristine potential of the new. If one was to describe a new power-generating technology with almost no pollution, practically limitless fuel supplies, reliable operations, scalable, and statistically far safer than existing alternatives, it would understandably sound like a miracle. Our energy needs would be solved. No wonder the early American advocates of nuclear fission were so excited. Experienced reality is always more complicated, of course. We should bring to bear this country's best minds and science and technologies to navigate that process responsibly. We have been through a roller-coaster on energy in this country that is not likely to stop. New challenges will emerge, as will new opportunities.

It is far too early to take nuclear off the table.

—Admiral James O. Ellis Jr., USN (ret.)

—George P. Shultz

Keeping the Lights on at America's Nuclear Power Plants

Jeremy Carl and David Fedor

Acknowledgments

We'd like to thank research, government, and industry representatives for their contributions to a May 2016 roundtable discussion convened at Stanford University's Hoover Institution. This work benefits from them in both concept and critique, though errors and opinions are those of the authors. We are further grateful to distinguished Energy Task Force members at Hoover, and particularly to its chairmen George P. Shultz and Thomas F. Stephenson, for their own continued guidance and support.

The Hoover Institution Shultz-Stephenson Task Force on Energy Policy's "Reinventing Nuclear Power" research series is edited by George P. Shultz and Admiral James O. Ellis, Jr., USN (ret). For more, please visit: www.hoover.org/reinventing-nuclear-power

Overview

Much has been made of shuttering coal power plants in this country, the victims of low-priced competition and increasingly stringent regulations. Those mourning the loss of these major polluters have been relatively few, if vocal. But coal is not alone. Nuclear power plants in the United States are closing or have been announced for closure at a historically unprecedented pace, too. Nuclear plants have no emissions, they are the cornerstone of America's central position in the global nuclear enterprise, and they are major capital investments, largely paid for by utility customers in decades past. What is going on here? While there are different proximate reasons for each closure, the deteriorating economic and regulatory environment in which these "silent giants" operate underlies each. Today's nuclear closures have outsized implications for America's energy future with respect to technology leadership, carbon emissions, and security.

There are four primary factors driving the decline of the existing nuclear fleet:

1. Naturally and artificially depressed wholesale electricity prices in deregulated states. This has been driven by an extended period of low natural gas prices with a large complementary stock of existing natural gas power plants; government production subsidies to renewables; and electricity market design issues that incentivize spot—but not baseload—power. Low wholesale prices are a good thing for consumers, but not if the market prices are lower than actual generation costs, which can occur if market participants are benefiting from out-of-market revenue streams (ultimately paid for by consumers through taxes or other levies). Nuclear must run 24/7 no matter the day-ahead or hour-ahead market pricing, which in some cases can now even be negative, so prices matter.

2. Loss of addressable market for nuclear generation over time in states with low electricity demand growth rates, high renewable power or efficiency mandates, or both.

3. A trend of high nuclear generation costs in older, smaller nuclear power plants and in nuclear plants requiring major refurbishment or upgrades. This trend occurs more broadly from a period of general operational and regulatory cost increases that have affected all plants.

4. Increasingly effective antinuclear advocacy efforts by both those who dislike nuclear power and those who see nuclear power as competition for their own favored forms of power generation.

Against these economic and financial pressures for nuclear, we are also witnessing a parallel megatrend: the development of increasingly ambitious state, national, and international targets to reduce greenhouse gas emissions. Many such plans put the onus for emission reductions squarely on the power generation sector. Nuclear power could significantly help, and is generally seen by experts as a desirable and even necessary component of any secure, low-carbon US power generation portfolio. When faced with outcry over cost or safety, nuclear advocates have long had a list of arguments ready in its defense: nuclear's grid reliability and scalability, its lack of pollution, and its supply chain and geopolitical implications. But the newly valuable attribute of zero carbon changes the nature of the nuclear question, resulting in political coalitions that may have been preposterous in years past.

The limited stock of the US nuclear fleet and the irreversible nature of any one plant closing therefore prompt a time-sensitive policy question: what steps, private and public, could be taken to mitigate nuclear closures? Importantly, such efforts would also be needed to support not just existing plants, but also the profitable operation and dispatch of any new-build US nuclear plants, whether using existing or upcoming advanced nuclear technologies. Here we examine a wide variety of those options and the entities who might enact them. Some policies would be more efficient or equitable than others. But politics is the realm of the possible, and that is more likely to be the ultimate arbiter of each.

State Public Utility Commissions (PUCs)

In states with traditionally regulated electricity market structures (in which twenty-nine of today's sixty nuclear plants reside), PUCs could support "uprates" (expansions of the maximum power level) at existing nuclear plants, which would improve overall plant profitability. Elsewhere, in deregulated states (representing thirty-one plants), PUCs could recognize the external environmental or economic values of nuclear plants by mandating the purchase of nuclear power by electricity distributors (as has been proposed in New York and Illinois) or by encouraging other above-current-market-rate long-term power purchase agreements, as was attempted in Ohio. More radically, PUCs in any state could require that intermittent power generators such as wind and solar bid into wholesale markets as "firmed energy" once a certain variable generation dispatch threshold is passed. This would likely raise the price of subsidized renewable generation that can otherwise drive down market prices below true cost.

State-Based Legislative Action

State lawmakers could establish nuclear portfolio standards or carveouts, or they could redefine renewables portfolio standards as technology-neutral zero-carbon portfolio standards, as Illinois once attempted to do. More broadly, they could increase the price of natural gas- and coal-fired generation by taxing or capping fossil fuel's carbon emissions.

Grid Operators

Electric grid regulators and operators—the Federal Energy Regulatory Commission (FERC), regional transmission organizations (RTOs), and independent system operators (ISOs)—could modify the wholesale electricity market and dispatch rules in ways that benefit nuclear power. These could include removing energy price caps and avoiding the use of uplift charges that limit energy prices, modifying capacity markets (for example by increasing their length terms), and addressing the phenomenon of negative wholesale power prices, which are exacerbated by the federal production tax credit (PTC) for wind power generation.

Environmental Protection Agency and Other Federal Agencies

The EPA could use its authority to regulate power sector carbon dioxide emissions by recognizing the carbon savings of power uprates at existing nuclear plants; or, more technically, individual states could fulfill any federal carbon goals through market mechanisms that generate a new revenue stream for existing nuclear plants. In addition, federal or state agencies could encourage the electrification of transportation, increasing the otherwise potentially stagnant national demand for electricity over time; more creatively, federal power agencies could take on long-term power purchase agreements for existing or new nuclear power plants, or themselves become stewards for temporarily suspended plants.

Congress

Members of Congress hold significant policy levers. They could overhaul the federal energy tax and subsidy regime, which in its current form favors other forms of electricity generation over nuclear power, by extending the renewables production tax credit (PTC) or investment tax credit (ITC) to nuclear power uprates, extending master limited partnership tax preferences to new nuclear power investment, or, alternately, reducing the existence of such distorting preferences as currently received by nuclear's competitors. In addition, as part of a much larger policy package, Congress could enact a broad-based revenue-neutral carbon tax that would recognize nuclear's emission-free power generation attributes, and for which it is currently almost universally not compensated.

Industry

Overall, governments have the most tools at their disposal to affect the viability of nuclear power. Given the degree of regulation in the electricity sector, much of this book therefore focuses on their role. But the nuclear research community and industry itself could also take technology development, investment, or operational steps to reduce the cost or increase the market value of nuclear generation from existing reactors. The electrical grid is likely to become increasingly intermittent, demand-responsive, and distributed. How will nuclear power play in this world?

- Plant owners could adopt a defensive budgetary stance, reducing capital outlays or operational spending to reduce overall generation costs.
- Operators could instead focus on improving revenues by continuing to increase existing reactor uptimes, potentially through the adoption of new fuels that require less frequent reloading.

- Operators could improve the operational flexibility of existing large nuclear reactors so that they can be dispatched in order to balance renewables on the grid, as is done in France and Germany but is almost unheard of domestically.
- Utilities or nuclear owners could increase investments in pumped hydro storage and other similar energy storage options or new transmission with the aim of joint operation that increases the flexibility (and value) of nuclear power dispatch into the grid.

Nuclear's supporters often point out that the US civilian nuclear industry confers a number of long-term *positive* externalities ranging from the local to international levels that are today largely taken for granted: environmental, industrial, technological, and geopolitical. The decision of which of the above pro-nuclear policy steps to pursue will need governments and regulators to first deliberate nuclear's value: value in both market and external social terms of existing or new nuclear plants within their jurisdictions, and value both now and as an option to preserve for the future. Ultimately, there are two potential paths for these or other interventions. One is the sweeping federal policy shift that changes fundamental operating conditions for nuclear or other similar large, baseload, low-carbon power technologies: adoption of a revenue-neutral carbon tax, for example. The other is a more locally oriented tapestry model that threads together some combination of these policy and operational options to fit both plant and state-level economic conditions and the desires of local constituencies and plant owners.

Finally, as we trace nuclear power's current struggles, we also uncover deeper strains in the broader American electricity market and regulatory apparatus during an unprecedented transformation amid rapid underlying technology changes. Specifically, many current electricity markets are geared toward incentivizing short-term cost minimization at the expense of long-term capital investments or portfolio diversity. Nuclear is not the first technology to run into this problem, and it is not likely to be the last. But its unique place in the American energy landscape could make it the one that finally forces the issue to the surface.

Admiral Hyman Rickover, credited as the father of the US nuclear power industry, once observed, "The Devil is in the details, but so is salvation." We offer the following in that spirit.

Recommendations for Policymakers

We are not nuclear advocates. We are not affiliated with or funded by the nuclear power industry. But we are analysts devoted to improving the nation's energy policies. There are many good policy improvements and energy technology options available to our country on energy going forward. We gradually became interested in the nuclear situation in part because we were surprised by the silence around it. While no technology is perfect, here was one that seemed to check many of the boxes of people from across ideological positions. And the data supports that. Yet we observed a sense of resignation among even the most equanimous in the energy field: nuclear was largely taken for granted, or outright ignored. It is a cognitive dissonance perhaps unique to nuclear.

We undertook this study because, on balance, we thought that the US nuclear power industry, even given its flaws, was one worth keeping the lights on for. The nuclear industry's challenges are real, and solutions to them are not perfect, but they are better than the status quo of no action.

So what should a policymaker with a will to change that do? We explore a number of possibilities in this book, any of which may be appropriate given the unique situations of various states and plant. But more broadly, we think that both shorter term patches and longer term fundamental reforms are warranted. We highlight some of the most important of these below:

- Two states have now demonstrated that guaranteeing medium-term supplementary revenue streams to existing nuclear plants through legislation or regulation can be done quickly, with bipartisan support, at a reasonable ratepayer cost, and are likely to pass federal scrutiny. Other states that wish to avoid the immediate disruption of plant shutdowns—whether they care about power markets, about local economies, or about pollution—should mimic those efforts

- Longer term, states should avoid heavily relying on renewable power generation quotas beyond moderate scales to guide electricity market development. Any requirement for one technology is also a prohibition on everything else. This gives lie to the underlying principle of competitive power markets.

And while states can do a lot to stop the bleeding, these second-best solutions are constrained by the national policy environment they operate in. So much of the value of the American nuclear power enterprise is not realized at the local level, so the obligation should not stay there either. The federal government therefore is justified in stepping in to further protect the broader American interests in security, in supply chains, and in international nuclear leadership:

- FERC should appreciate that it no longer simply plays the role of impartial power market referee—it has involved itself directly in the relative competitiveness of nuclear and other power generation technologies and should own up to that reality in how it conducts itself, or change its charter.
- Congress should similarly recognize the damage it has enabled to nuclear economics through years of selective, politically-expedient subsidies to competing technologies. Nuclear power should first be brought to par as part of deal that then gradually rolls back these preferences across the board to zero—getting taxpayer money out of the day-to-day energy business.
- Meanwhile, federal power agencies and national labs have the unique ability to extend the viability of nuclear plants by taking novel responsibilities for them—such as facilitating temporary plant suspensions as needed, or entering into long-term power purchasing agreements—that the private sector cannot. The White House can afford the broadest strategic vision on such matters and should direct the agencies to evaluate such initiatives through its bully pulpit.

> In sum we believe that the United States will be putting itself in a weaker position if we permanently opt out of the nuclear enterprise. Luckily there are steps that we know can avoid this. We should undertake these measures, and others as necessary, the ensure that nuclear remains and important part of a diverse and resilient American energy mix.

Introduction

Today, about 59 percent of America's zero carbon power comes from nuclear plants (EIA 2016a). Studies from across the ideological spectrum recognize a dramatically increased role for nuclear power generation in order to hit aggressive carbon dioxide emission reduction targets. But today's existing US nuclear plants are closing down and reactor uprates (expansions of maximum power levels) are being abandoned. Out of approximately one hundred commercial nuclear reactors in America, five have been shuttered since 2009, another seven are announced or likely for closure, and fifteen to twenty reactors are considered to be at near-term closure risk.[1] And while new nuclear power technologies look promising, developing a new nuclear industrial supply chain will depend heavily on the foundation provided by America's current nuclear workforce's expertise and regulatory experience. Moreover, even those technologies will have to succeed up against similar market and policy challenges.

Nuclear power has innate characteristics that merit special considerations and business strategies so that it can remain a viable form of electricity generation, and this study addresses that. But it is also important to recognize that nuclear power's current struggles are also a symptom of deeper injury within the United States' power market investment and regulatory decision-making process. A patchwork of half-liberalized market structures and overlapping regulatory organs at different levels of

---

1.   The estimate of at-risk plants comes from the Nuclear Energy Institute (NEI), the
      US civilian nuclear power trade organization.

government, already stretched to its limit during times of normal operation, has now collided with a barrage of ambitious laws and policy goals aimed at wholesale transformation of the energy system. Holding this ship together—not just for nuclear but for other new energy technologies as well—will likely require a reconciliation process that is only now becoming visible on the horizon.

Amid high public support for reducing carbon emissions and a continued need for domestic nuclear expertise in both the civilian and military sectors, what are America's options as it faces a changing nuclear landscape?

This study answers that question by looking at a menu of changes that could be made *relative to the status quo* and by characterizing the implications of those options. Each of them occupies essentially one of two overarching approaches: (1) make nuclear power cost less for a given benefit, or otherwise use external subsidies to reduce its nominal price; or (2) make nuclear power's competitors cost more for a given benefit, or otherwise reduce the use of existing subsidies that reduce their nominal prices. Whether any of these options should be pursued therefore becomes a matter of judgment in deciding—and convincing the general public—about the unique environmental, security, or economic benefits that nuclear power offers to a rapidly changing US electrical grid.

It is important to recognize that the options taken to address nuclear power's viability must address how this technology will continue to function *alongside increased deployment of natural gas, renewables, other low-carbon technologies, energy efficiency, customer demand response, and distributed generation or other emerging distribution grid technologies.* In most areas of the United States, public support is extremely strong for renewables and efficiency; policy has followed that to ensure that these technologies will be a cornerstone of the future grid. Though the implementation details, pace, and ultimate levels of adoption will vary based upon cost and consumer acceptance, the basic direction has been set. The answer to nuclear's current woes can therefore not be how to reverse this, but rather how to ensure (1) that global warming-driven support for renewables and efficiency does not inadvertently result in the closure of nuclear plants, which provide even more valuable zero carbon power,

(2) that despite being a mature technology, nuclear is able to compete on a fair field that values its actual benefits, and (3) that the nuclear industry finds new ways to maximize the system value of its technologies to a changing grid in ways that complement gas, renewables and distributed resources. Moreover, to paraphrase the late Steve Jobs, today's nuclear industry has to let go of the notion that for nuclear to win, gas or renewables have to lose. Instead, it has to embrace the notion that for nuclear to win, nuclear has to do a really good job. What are the policy options then that could allow this competition to play out on a level field?

Nuclear Power, Washington Politics, and Climate Math

Would nuclear power be needed to reach United States' decarbonization goals? As part of international agreements, the Obama administration formally adopted greenhouse gas emission reduction targets of 26–28 percent below 2005 levels by the year 2025; though the Trump administration is not likely to continue them, the business community is likely to hedge its bets against a future Democratic takeover and thus continue them at least to some degree. However, some states have taken on even more aggressive emission mitigation targets through gubernatorial executive orders or legislation: these targets will largely be unaffected by which party controls Washington, DC. Such reductions would entail a significant restructuring of today's energy economy, including substantial changes to the power sector, which is today responsible for 30 percent of US greenhouse gas emissions (Herndon and Larsen 2016). Given the scale of these changes, a number of studies have attempted to model potential power generation mixes that could achieve such goals while supplying a growing economy.

A recent technical analysis undertaken by the Department of Energy's national lab **Pathways to Deep Decarbonization** project (Williams et al. 2014), for example, found that 80 percent reductions of US greenhouse gas emissions by 2050 were technically feasible, if at a significant cost. In each scenario, nuclear continued to play an important role alongside renewables, carbon capture and storage (CCS), efficiency, and other technologies—ranging from 9.6 percent to 40.3 percent of US electricity generation in 2050 (with the lowest overall costs most likely in scenarios in which nuclear power generation grows from today).

Stanford University's **Energy Modeling Forum** convenes independent groups of international energy and climate modelers to explore similar policy questions. In their 2014 meeting, nine teams used different tools to evaluate scenarios in which 50 percent or 80 percent of US decarbonization goals were pursued with or without the development of large-scale low-carbon baseload power generation sources such as nuclear or carbon capture (EMF24 2014). A number of technology mixes were deemed technically possible, but with significantly different economic and social impacts. For hypothetical futures where nuclear and carbon capture technologies were made more available, a number of models across this meta-analysis indicated significantly lower total system carbon abatement costs and electricity prices, with greater production of electricity. Removing the nuclear option increased total social costs of meeting a given emission target and reduced the long-term electrification potential of the vehicle fleet, or alternately reduced the amount of total emission reductions delivered for a given carbon price level. One model, for example, estimated that given a phaseout of nuclear power, a national carbon price would have to increase by 33 percent more in order to achieve a 50 percent greenhouse gas emission reduction by 2050.

Following Governor Jerry Brown's 2005 Executive Order S-3–05, which set a target of 80 percent emissions reductions below 1990 levels in California, a **California Council on Science and Technology** expert group was commissioned to evaluate potential pathways for the state to reach these goals, considering both technical and economic factors (CCST 2011). Acknowledging cost and technological uncertainties, the group found that the state could attain 60 percent emission reductions with existing technologies given aggressive improvements in energy efficiency, electrification, and complete decarbonization of the electricity sector—using an equal mix of nuclear, renewables, and natural gas with carbon capture—alongside a doubling in electricity production. Eighty percent reductions further required the scaled deployment of not-yet-available technologies such as economical zero emission storage/load balancing technologies (such as large batteries) or hydrogen infrastructures (created by zero emission power sources). The group therefore indicated that the state should prepare the legislative framework to significantly build out its nuclear power fleet alongside continued growth in renewable power generation.

A recent analysis from the **Rhodium Group** (Larsen, Herndon, and Larsen 2016) examined the impacts of nuclear retirements in the context of the Obama administration's enacted and proposed power sector policies. The analysts found that over three-quarters of lost generation from nearly two dozen at-risk nuclear power plants in the United States would be replaced by fossil generation, largely natural gas combined-cycle technology. In all scenarios, these retirements would increase pollution and carbon dioxide emissions, offsetting significant portions of mitigation gains otherwise delivered under the EPA plan or otherwise accelerating total sector emissions. Similarly, a late-2016 Department of Energy (DOE) **Energy Information Administration** review found that following recent nuclear plant closures in California and Florida, lost generation was replaced primarily by natural gas; lost nuclear generation in Wisconsin was replaced by coal; lost generation in Vermont was replaced by unspecified out-of-state imports; and lost nuclear generation in Nebraska is expected to be made up by natural gas and wind (EIA 2016b).

Diagnosing the Situation Today

While critics of nuclear power generation often focus on potential safety, waste disposal, fuel availability, or construction and financing costs, these issues do not feature among the most pressing concerns for operating civilian nuclear power reactors today. In fact, there is not one simple explanation for today's nuclear closures. Rather, we can see that different plants in different regions of the country face bundles of challenges, some generalizable and some idiosyncratic. What is notable about these challenges is that many of them are essentially new developments. Importantly though, many of them can be reduced to the prosaic common denominator that they negatively affect day-to-day or year-to-year economics of actually operating a nuclear plant.

Every technology or power portfolio strategy has intrinsic weaknesses and strengths. Nuclear, however, finds itself today with a confluence of unexpected hurdles to its basic operational business case in addition to its other well-known special characteristics or conspicuous existential considerations. Below we explore problems affecting plants in a variety of different situations.

Plants operating in deregulated states (e.g., Midwest Independent System Operator or PJM Interconnection territories) are increasingly challenged in their ability to dispatch generation into competitive electricity markets where hourly clearing prices increasingly fall below even a fully capital-depreciated plant's operating costs. Thirty-one of the country's sixty plants (operating forty-nine of one hundred reactors) now operate in "deregulated" states, where the plant's power is sold to electricity distributors (and ultimately end-consumers) in a competitive fashion such that profit is not guaranteed to the plant owner, as it might be to a traditionally vertically integrated utility.[2] While exact market price dynamics vary by region, this means that nuclear operators are competing directly against power generation technologies with marginal generation costs that are often equal to or lower than those of existing plants, including wind, solar, and natural gas-based generation. As a result, many nuclear operators now report that plants are losing money on an annual basis.

This issue is mostly concentrated in the Midwest, Mid-Atlantic, and Northeast states. For example, the average market-clearing price for a

---

2. While the Energy Information Administration describes the Duane Arnold Energy Center in Iowa and Point Beach Nuclear Plant in Wisconsin as operating in traditionally regulated states, they are considered here as operating in deregulated environments due to those plants' reliance on power purchase agreements for generation sales. See Barua, Keogh, and Phelan (2015), writing for the National Association of Regulatory Utility Commissioners (NARUC) for further discussion of the impacts of regulatory environment on existing nuclear power plants.

megawatt-hour of electricity sold in the Midwest Independent System Operator (MISO) territory in 2015 was about $28 (including both "energy" and smaller "capacity" charges). Within the PJM Interconnection regional transmission organization, which extends across thirteen Mid-Atlantic and Appalachian states, it was $47, and in New England it was $54 (Phillips 2016). These prices are historically low—the lowest in two decades in even nominal terms—and are driven by four things: (1) low levels of growth in demand for power, a combination of aggressive energy efficiency programs, industrial shifts into less energy-intensive activities, and overall slow macroeconomic growth rates; (2) historically low natural gas prices resulting from the US shale gas revolution, which as the main cost component of natural gas-fired power generation in turn drives down generation costs; (3) general overcapacity in power generation infrastructure, with a number of depreciated thermal power plants, including coal and natural gas merchant plants built up rapidly during the peak of deregulation in the 1990s; and (4) in some areas, rapid growth in wind power generation, which has almost zero marginal operating costs and which also receives a federal government production tax credit (over its first ten years of operation) of approximately $23 per megawatt-hour. Nuclear utilities have pointed out that this incentivizes wind operators to continue dispatching power even when regional grid prices are *negative*, as the production tax credit allows them to still turn a profit in such situations. Compounding this is the fact that the best wind resources often occur at night, the time of day with the lowest electricity demand and a traditional mainstay of nuclear power's 24/7 baseload operating regime. In fact, the nuclear utility Exelon reports that in 2015, 14 percent of all hours in its territory faced negative prices (i.e., the generator must pay distributors in order to dispatch its power).[3]

Against this backdrop, the Nuclear Energy Institute (NEI), the nuclear industry's advocacy organization, reports that US nuclear generation costs

---

3. The wind industry's trade association has contested this figure, arguing that this percentage refers only to the share of off-peak hours facing negative pricing. "Who's to Blame for Negative Prices? Wind Generators: We're not nukes' problem," *RTO Insider*, April 22, 2014.

today average $36 per megawatt-hour, ranging from $29 in the best performing quartile to $44 in the worst (Phillips 2016). This figure suggests that plant-by-plant costs are quite inconsistent, the result of region, owner/ operator, and plant age and design characteristics. It also suggests that a portion of US nuclear plants should be able to operate profitably even in today's very low-price environments. But it clearly points to the fact that a significant portion of currently operating nuclear plants is losing money. Exelon, the nation's largest nuclear plant owner, again reports that across its portfolio of twenty-four units in seven states, sixteen are currently not recovering the costs of operation, with its Illinois plants— Clinton and Quad Cities—losing a combined $800 million since 2010.[4] As one example, in New York State, home to six units across four plants, nuclear plants were able to receive a market-clearing price exceeding average generation costs for just 20–30 percent of total operating hours in 2015.

Since the advent of deregulation, US nuclear plants have represented a risky but potentially lucrative generation bet for their owners. With essentially low and (in the case of any one plant) stable operating costs, they reap a windfall (and help suppress customer energy costs) when electricity market prices are high, such as they were amid high natural gas and coal prices in the mid-2000s. In fact, many of the nuclear portfolios of competitive generators today were amassed through purchase or acquisitions during that period with these same market expectations. But when markets are low, as today, continued operation can represent a large cash-flow burden—a sort of levered bet that market prices will rise in the future. An obvious answer to the situation might simply be to let the market play itself out and wait for prices to recover through a rise in overall demand or exit of supply. This has been done with gas, coal, and even oil-fired power plants historically in this country and elsewhere. Nuclear power, though, inserts an important additional caveat—nuclear plants cannot be mothballed and later brought back online when needed.

---

4. Rebecca Smith, "Exelon Moves to Close Two Illinois Nuclear Plants," *Wall Street Journal*, June 2, 2016.

Essentially, once they are shut down and begin the expensive de-fueling and decommissioning process, they will not come back.[5] One strategic calculus for policymakers—or owners—is then to decide if the current market conditions represent an aberration from the natural state, and so temporary costs should be incurred to retain the option value of nuclear power, or if in fact the current low-price market can be expected to persist over the long term, meaning that a subsidy to nuclear power generation could turn out to be open-ended.

Single-unit or small plants magnify most of the other economic challenges that face nuclear power in the current market. Because significant amounts of the operating costs for current plant designs are fixed (e.g., perimeter security, administrative, regulatory, and some staffing), costs per megawatt-hour of production tend to rise as the number of annually dispatchable megawatt-hours from each plant decreases. The hurdle rate for profitability on these plants is higher than for sites with two or more units, which is the norm; twenty-five nuclear plants in the United States operating today are single units, versus thirty-five plants with multiple units. NEI estimates that single-unit sites in the United States have average generation costs exceeding $44 per megawatt-hour, versus $33 for multiunit sites. This calculus has been a factor in five recent or scheduled plant closures (and underscores the industry's current and future focus on multiunit deployments).

Looking forward, it is important that this phenomenon of higher operating costs at lower scales be carefully considered against the prospects

---

5. Current nuclear licensing rules limit power plants to existing in one of three states: construction, operation, and decommissioning. One recent proposal has therefore been to develop a strategic nuclear power reserve "fourth state" in which the US government would assume caretaker responsibilities for uneconomical plants that private operators wish to shutter. The plants would be de-fueled and provided with basic equipment maintenance and security for a period of five to ten years, at a cost of a few tens of millions of dollars annually. The utility would maintain ultimate plant decommissioning responsibilities as well as a call option to reassume plant control and bring it back into operation were electricity market conditions to change.

for promising new nuclear technologies such as potential light water-based small modular nuclear reactors (SMRs), which would have reactor sizes of less than about 100 megawatts-electric but could be theoretically manufactured at scale in factory settings. There are similarities and key differences. SMRs, for example, aim to reduce operating costs despite their small size in part due to lower absolute construction costs/risk and in part due to design elements such as undergrounding, streamlined refueling, or shared control rooms. Today's experience with profitably operating smaller conventional light water reactors (many of them still five to ten times the size of envisioned SMRs) illustrates the importance of meeting these design (and regulatory) goals to accommodate potential future SMR viability.

Plants in low load growth, high renewables target states (which may also share some of the other challenging attributes above) face a less immediate but nevertheless existential situation. Twenty-nine states have implemented renewables portfolio standards (RPS), but none of them include nuclear power within their definition of "renewable." Modest RPS targets are not a direct threat to nuclear power's market viability. But as targets have risen, to as high as 50 percent in some states, nuclear operators face a regulatory environment in which an increasing share of the consumption base is essentially made off-limits for their product—for both existing and potential new capacity. While it is likely not the intent of RPS policies to hurt the viability of nuclear power, it has resulted in unforeseen conflicts between the two forms of power.

Recently, in California, for example, plant owner Pacific Gas and Electric (PG&E) announced a plan to not seek a license extension of a currently profitable and generally well-performing nuclear plant in part because of legislation in that state which requires a high share of renewable power. In that case, models indicated that meeting the state's renewables targets would result in midday over-generation of solar power, depressing hourly market prices for power toward zero during a traditionally profitable period of the day.[6] The high renewables target threatened

6. Gavin Bade, "After Diablo Canyon: PG&E CEO Tony Earley on Renewables, DERs and California's Energy Future," *Utility Dive*, June 30, 2016.

to undermine the economics of the existing nuclear plant; on the flip side of the coin, shuttering the nuclear plant would potentially improve the profitability of the already-legislated renewables build-out. Perversely, current market structures may therefore be incentivizing renewables supporters to support the closure of nuclear plants.[7]

Of course, the impact of a declining share of a power market due to renewables mandates would be less important if the overall market were growing in size due to rising demand. In many areas of the country, however, electricity demand growth was flat—with essentially no growth in sales nationwide between 2007 and 2014 (EIA 2016c). Most states in 2014 had less than 0.5 percent growth in electricity sales.[8] Overall, the EIA expects US electricity sales to rise by only 0.7 percent annually through 2040, with the economic intensity of electricity use falling in every sector (EIA 2016c). The fate of the US nuclear industry has long been tied to expectations about growth in power demand, with utilities in the 1960s famously projecting load growth that would have today put consumption orders a magnitude above actual use (Craig, Gadgil, and Koomey 2002). The sudden arrival of an energy efficiency mind-set following the 1970s oil crises was responsible for a structural change in the trajectory of US electricity demand (Sweeney 2016). And today, energy efficiency measures are adopted through both market forces and regulation: in addition to federal efficiency standards for appliances, most states regularly update building energy codes, and twenty-six states have adopted formal power sector "energy efficiency resource standards" that mandate overall efficiency gains (Bingaman et al. 2014).

---

7. A comprehensive state utility-funded study analyzing costs and options for California to increase its RPS standard from 33 to 50 percent in 2030 (a goal which was later passed into law by the legislature) estimated that statewide electricity prices would increase from 9–23 percent as a result. With existing nuclear power retained in the state's system, the increased renewables investment delivered carbon dioxide abatement at an implied cost ranging from $403 to $1,020 per ton (Energy and Environmental Economics 2014).

8. One exception to this, as with many of the other challenges outlined here, is in the Southeast, where electricity demand continues to grow faster than the national average.

As with the broader market price challenges described above, a key question for nuclear's viability—particularly new plants—will be whether the current low load growth rates are a new normal for the United States or if they are a temporary aberration resulting from a sluggish recovery from the financial crisis. One highly uncertain but extremely important variable in this calculus is the extent to which the US transportation system will or will not become electrified in coming decades. With only marginal penetration of electric vehicles to date, there is currently an intellectual disconnect between, on the one hand, aggressive deployment subsidies and targets for electric vehicles from the federal government and many states and, on the other hand, electricity sector planning scenarios that do not necessarily accept that these targets will be met. The extent—and timing—of that transition would probably be the most important organic answer to the nuclear question, but it is one not yet able to be banked.

Plants facing new investment needs or refurbishment costs, whether due to unforeseen repairs or upgrades and uprates, have an additional hurdle layered on top of those described above. Uprates and improvements in US nuclear fleet capacity factors—from 66 percent in 1990 to over 92 percent in 2015—have added the annual generation equivalent of thirty stand-alone reactors (EIA 2016d). But at least eleven major planned capacity uprates have now been postponed or abandoned by US nuclear operators since 2011.[9] Uprates, which add electric production to an existing plant where technically feasible, can be an attractive option for owners who see them as a way to increase plant sales and revenues without substantively incurring new operating costs.[10] Uprates do, however, incur onetime capital, regulatory, and other administrative costs.

---

9. These include planned capacity expansions for reactors at Browns Ferry, Alabama; Clinton, Illinois; LaSalle, Illinois; Limerick, Pennsylvania; Oconee, South Carolina; and Three Mile Island, Pennsylvania. "Exelon cancels power uprates for LaSalle, Limerick nuclear plants," *S&P Global Platts*, June 12, 2013.

10. Main categories of nuclear uprates include, in increasing order of cost and impact: measurement uncertainty recapture (upgrading instrumentation precisions to allow operating performance closer to tolerances); stretch uprates (getting more

The uprate decisions can be thought of somewhat similarly to operating license extensions from forty to sixty years: they are dependent on the owner's assessment of the profitability of that decision given the associated up-front costs.

For regulated owners, rate-basing these costs would generally need to be approved by convincing the state's public utility commission of their ultimate value to end-use customers, weighed against other options (such as energy efficiency or new nonnuclear forms of generation). Owners in competitive markets, on the other hand, would have to internally determine their expected rate of return over time for such investments given market energy prices or other potential streams of income. In recent years, uprates have been postponed or abandoned across both such environments.

Most of the country's current civilian nuclear fleet was commissioned between 1970 and 1990; refurbishment of components such as generators, turbines, and piping is becoming more common as components age and as plants anticipate or receive operating license extensions to sixty years. Recent experience suggests, however, that this process has become more *financially* risky as a combination of weak overall market economics; antinuclear public advocacy that reduces tolerance for cost overruns; or greater-than-anticipated engineering challenges. Even plants in regulated environments (where plant operators may be able to pass along many of their refurbishment costs to a captive customer base) have run into severe challenges. In Florida, an economical plant at Crystal River was shut in 2013 following a failed repair job that would have required significant sums of money to mend. While a repair was technically feasible and deemed safe, the operator, against a backdrop of negative public opinion, lost the confidence of the regulator and was not permitted to recover the needed costs (despite a likely positive overall benefit-cost trade-off in doing so). In a similar situation, two units of the San Onofre Nuclear Generating Station on the coast of Southern California faced

---

from existing equipment); and extended power uprates (which can include the replacement of major plant subsystems such as turbines or generators).

extended shutdown in 2012 due to component wear stemming from a faulty turbine replacement in one of the reactors. Facing public opposition, Southern California Edison, the operating utility, abandoned the reactor with the bad turbine and later also abandoned the second reactor unit at that plant, citing, in part, the poor anticipated economics of operating a single unit. While both these examples are to some degree idiosyncratic, they also illustrate how systematic issues have in parallel unexpectedly constrained the option space available to the US nuclear power industry in such situations, further reducing overall margins for error and increasing financial risk.

License Extensions

While forty-year to sixty-year operating license extensions were, up until recently, seen as a potential barrier to nuclear power's continued operation in the United States, the process has been relatively smooth overall. Every plant that is still operating or not announced for closure and which is nearing its license expiration has successfully received a license extension (fifty plants in total, including those which have subsequently shuttered); is under review (eight plants); or is expected to apply for an extension (four plants). The process has, however, resulted in major challenges at some plants. The Pilgrim Nuclear Power Station in Massachusetts faced major opposition and litigation from various advocacy groups (safety, environmental, and others) during its extension application and took more than six years to receive approval from a split commission. The single-unit plant was subsequently announced for closure despite successfully receiving NRC approval. At the Limerick, Pennsylvania, nuclear plant, license extensions were delayed by legal intervenors on matters such as on-site capacity for dry cask storage of spent fuel, given the lack of a federal long-term nuclear waste repository.

The NRC is developing guidance for sixty-year to eighty-year "subsequent license renewals" and two operators—Dominion Power at its two-unit Surry, Virginia, plant and Exelon at its two-unit Peach Bottom,

Pennsylvania, plant—have so far announced their intent to pursue that, from 2019. Costs for these extensions may be significant given the potential but yet undetermined need to upgrade cabling, aspects of the reactor vessel, and containment buildings due to any age-related materials degradation.

Plants in states with influential antinuclear advocacy face additional pressures. While antinuclear advocacy has long been a factor in the nuclear industry, and the industry has developed its own responses to it, there have been a few recent changes. First is that, following years of apparent detente, those set against nuclear power have been animated by both the new financial challenges faced by the industry and the promise of a partial alternative to nuclear power's own low emissions profile in the cost declines of solar and wind power. This was seen in the recently announced proposed closure of California's Diablo Canyon nuclear power plant, where national environmental groups negotiated a deal with the utility owner—to "replace" the station with additional renewable power deployment—before any discussions with the state regulator or customers took place.[11]

Second is the apparent failure of nuclear power to win public "mindspace" within the climate change movement. Despite strong support for

---

11. Describing his apparent success in the decades-long campaign against Diablo Canyon Nuclear Power Plant, prominent activist (and former Tennessee Valley Authority chairman) John Freeman of the antinuclear organization Friends of the Earth in late 2016 dismissed nuclear's low-carbon characteristics, saying, "Just because a person is a climatologist does not mean he knows a damn thing about the dangers of nuclear power. There are the carbon-only environmentalists, and they're a threat to mankind. . . . We've got to replace every damn fossil fuel plant in the country over the next thirty years, and here [the Diablo Canyon shutdown plan] is a green yardstick for doing it. I would think that if we're serious about not all moving to the North Pole, every damn coal plant and nuclear plant in the country should be given this treatment." Debra Kahn, "Anti-Nuclear Movement Set Its Sight on Calif. Closures," *E&E News*, December 2016.

carbon dioxide emission reductions—78 percent of Americans support government policies to force US "business" to reduce greenhouse gas emissions (Krosnick 2015)—and the potential that nuclear power would therefore benefit from new emission mitigation policies or regulations, the industry has seen little benefit in the way that renewable energy, efficiency, or even natural gas power generation has.[12] While some states could be said to indirectly aid nuclear power due to its inclusion in regulated rate bases, no state has instituted a "nuclear portfolio standard," deployment targets, feed-in tariffs, or tax credits, as has been done for a variety of other low-carbon generation or energy efficiency resources in the name of climate policy. Meanwhile, at the federal level, the Obama administration EPA's proposed Clean Power Plan, despite some minor beneficial proposal revisions, did not effectively encourage the development of new nuclear plants or lifetime extensions of existing plants. In civil society, no major mainstream US environmental advocacy group has openly endorsed nuclear power as a needed component of a low-carbon power generation portfolio. Following a period of brief reconsideration, groups such as the Natural Resources Defense Council and the Sierra Club, as well as some popular academics, now appear to be forcefully rejecting the nuclear power option. And when polled, just 36 percent of the US public currently favors giving tax breaks to companies to build nuclear power plants, versus 80 percent who favor the same for water, wind, and solar power facilities (Krosnick 2015).

Finally, despite the efforts of various nuclear industry advocacy groups, public education on nuclear power's climate attributes remains poor. When polled, only 25 percent of Americans stated a belief that nuclear power does not emit greenhouse gases, versus 67 percent who believed nuclear to emit either "a little" (44 percent) or "a lot" (23 percent) (Bisconti 2014).[13] Seventy percent of those polled did not correctly

---

12. See poll figures at www.rff.org/files/sharepoint/Documents/RFF-NYTimes -Stanford-global-warming-poll-Jan-2015-topline.pdf.

13. For comparison, 50 percent of those polled in the same survey said they believed hydropower emitted no greenhouse gases, 77 percent thought the same for wind, and 71 percent for solar.

identify nuclear as the country's largest low-carbon power source among listed choices (Bisconti 2015). The general public's lack of knowledge about nuclear power likely contributes to susceptibility to emotion-based appeals or simply its broader invisibility in the political consciousness. With just sixty (generally isolated) physical power plant locations nationwide, and twenty states with zero plants, there is little natural opportunity to improve nuclear's salience versus more visible power generation technologies.[14] Notably, public knowledge and perceptions of nuclear power markedly improve among individuals who have visited nuclear plants in person or who live near them.

But not all new challenges are purely external. A trend of rising generation costs (combined fuel, capital, and operating costs) further weakens the economics in many existing nuclear plants. NEI estimates that average US nuclear fleet costs, in real terms, rose from $28 per megawatt-hour in 2002 to over $36 in 2014, having first reached $40 in 2012. These costs are driven by the implementation of $3 billion in Nuclear Regulatory Commission-mandated antiterrorism capital expenditures and additional security staffing; a 25 percent real increase in fuel costs; and license extension investments and increased general maintenance needs of aging equipment. In response, the industry in 2015 adopted an effort to cut average costs back to $28 per megawatt-hour by 2020[15] through issuance of a series of "efficiency bulletins" to operators that recommend, for example, slowing capital expenditure, reducing non-maintenance staff overhead or high-cost but noncritical preventative maintenance items, improving training programs, adopting more efficient inspection practices, and using contract forensics (NEI 2016). Fuel costs are also expected to decline in the short term given global reactor shutdowns in

---

14. Social interaction (so-called "peer" or "neighborhood effects") have been shown to be powerful influencers of knowledge about, and potentially support for, other clean energy technologies, such as rooftop solar panels (Bollinger and Gillingham 2012).

15. Categorically, the target breaks down to a $6.50 per megawatt-hour savings in capital expenditures, $3.50 in operations and maintenance, and $2 in fuel savings.

Japan and Germany. [16] Though these efforts may yield improvements in the cost-effectiveness of existing plants, it is of course very important that they do not result in meaningful reductions in the safety of the US nuclear fleet. The United States provides a valuable but uncompensated global service today in the quality of its operators and nuclear institutions, both public and nonprofit, regarding the norms, procedures, and rules they enact and offer up as a de facto international gold standard. This should be preserved. At the same time, this fleet must remain viable if it is to exist as a convincing model to current or aspiring nuclear operators and regulators globally.

The $28 cost-cutting target represents a level that many in the industry view as a reasonable competitiveness target, especially in comparison to natural gas, but it is not a panacea: in the Texas power market, for example, grid energy prices are currently closer to $26 per megawatt-hour, and there are few mechanisms such as the capacity charges that benefit nuclear operators in most other regions. Assuming that the industry is able to successfully forgo new or extended cyclical capital expenditures, especially following the post-Fukushima security-related uptick, viability of the broader cost-cutting goal will hinge on the ability to manage day-to-day operational costs. [17] Meanwhile, it is also useful to consider trends in nuclear generation costs against the more extreme variability exhibited by baseload alternatives such as natural gas combined-cycle generation: just in Texas, for example, EIA (2016c) reports that the price of natural gas delivered to utility power plants has either doubled or been cut in half at least five times since 2008, heavily contributing to overall price volatility within those power portfolios.

Just as bonds are valued in portfolios for their lower but more predictable returns than equities, nuclear power should be valued by electricity

---

16. Hannah Northey and Kristi Swartz, "Nuclear: 'We're Not Going to Cost Cut Our Way Out of This Problem,'" *E&E News*, July 25, 2016.

17. One additional cost faced by some nuclear plants is grid transmission congestion, which results in congestion fees that can range from $5 to $10 per megawatt-hour (UBS 2016). These are not necessarily nuclear-specific, however.

generator portfolios for its predictable cost and generation attributes, even if it is not always the short-run cheapest solution.

In summary, many existing reactors face at least one or some combination of these challenges, to varying degrees of intensity. It is important to note that some reactors nonetheless remain profitable despite these headwinds, or are even insulated entirely—particularly, if not universally, in traditionally regulated states where rates of return are essentially guaranteed or for newer, large, multiple reactor plants in regions with high average grid prices. For any potential intervention in the US nuclear power industry or markets, there is the possibility that one plant's lifeline could be another's windfall.

Moreover, this is not the first time in modern history that the US nuclear industry has seen viability challenges: the 1990s saw the closure of ten nuclear reactors, but overall production levels (and profits) nevertheless managed to stay robust, in part through more efficient and intensive use of existing assets. As the obvious headroom for such organic replenishment tops out, however, and the impact of carbon dioxide emissions becomes more salient, the question remains whether different policy reforms or support steps can or should be taken today. The rest of this study explores what options might be available to do so.

New Nuclear vs. Existing Nuclear

One important distinction worth addressing up front is the matter of new versus existing nuclear plants. The "nuclear renaissance" envisioned during the mid-2000s entailed the development of a number of new nuclear power plants using updated but largely technologically known "Gen III+" designs such as the Toshiba-Westinghouse AP1000 pressurized light water reactor, of which four units are now in construction at two American sites. In parallel, nuclear researchers and technology vendors have prototyped or otherwise outlined more radical nuclear power generation technologies, including both the smaller "integral" factory-built light water reactors known as small modular reactors and the advanced but not yet commercially available "Gen IV" large reactor concepts such as molten-salt, very-high-temperature, gas-cooled, or pebble bed reactors. Gen III+, SMRs, and Gen IV nuclear technologies each has its own development and deployment challenges, potential policy options, and relevant timelines. Independent of these special risks and barriers to commercialization, however, is the additional fact that any new nuclear plant would likely face very similar day-to-day electricity market dispatch challenges as the country's existing nuclear fleet does. Though new nuclear technologies aim to avoid by design some of the troubles faced by today's existing fleet (going so far as to, in some cases, produce only industrial process heat rather than grid electric power), they cannot completely absolve the current operating environment. The issues discussed in this study can therefore be thought of as applying to both existing and new plants—solving them being a necessary, but not sufficient, task before allowing any new nuclear technology deployment.

Policy and Regulatory Options

Because changing the status quo for nuclear will require that choices be made, we have organized this menu of policy options according to those who will face them, starting from those governing bodies closest to these plants.

State regulatory commissions could make customers pay more for nuclear or nuclear-style generation, arguing that it has special or newly desirable attributes.

The most significant electricity sector policy and regulation decisions occur at the state level. Public utility commissions, also referred to as public service commissions, are generally the primary actors: long-lived bodies, often with independent or quasi-constitutional powers, directed by a board of commissioners either elected or appointed by the governor. They are empowered to set the rules by which vertically integrated monopoly utilities (in traditional "regulated" states) or electricity distributors and retailers or other power producers (in reformed "deregulated" states) do business. They also often act as system-wide planning bodies, are arbiters of system risk and reliability, set electricity consumer rates as well as profit margins for regulated utilities, and can be charged with implementing broad directives and goals handed down from the state legislatures. In short, they have both power and flexibility in shaping a state's electricity system.

States with Traditionally Regulated Environments

State regulatory commissions could choose to encourage nuclear power generation by developing various mechanisms to direct more ratepayer money toward it. In most regulated states with monopoly utilities, such bodies already have broad discretion to do so, with public support (or intervenor lawsuits) as the primary moderating factor to ensure that such decisions are made in the public interest. While a regulated nuclear utility has to provide an economic basis for its proposed investments, including an evaluation of alternatives, there is substantial asymmetry in anticipated cost, benefit, and investment risk information between a monopoly utility and its regulator. Moreover, it may not be possible to definitively argue the optimization of "public interest."

In some states, such as Washington, the definition can be more objective: cost minimization. Elsewhere, though, the target can be more value-laden: diversity, reliability, etc. In Mississippi, for example, the public service commission's decision criterion is to enable the state's "economic development." In either case, the regulator's influence comes down to its support or rejection of various proposed nuclear investments through a "prudence review" or the conditions it applies to such investments that could affect their desirability. The primary vehicles for such decisions include the periodic regulator-driven "integrated resource planning" process, which provides a road map for a state's electricity development and can take into account current and future customer electricity demand trends, technological availability, fuel prices, grid infrastructure needs, reliability, overall costs, and investment risks. Utilities can also approach regulators with individual proposed investments or as part of periodic required broader bundled "rate cases" which evaluate overall utility costs and allowed profits.

Recent examples include a series of uprates totaling 522 megawatts across four reactors under Florida Power and Light's ownership: the utility won approval to pass on the $3.4 billion cost of this program from the traditionally regulated state's Public Service Commission, completing the work in 2013 (Florida PSC 2014). A 2006 Florida law furthermore authorized the commission to let Florida Power and Light capitalize the work in progress, meaning that customer rates were increased to cover expenses during construction, as opposed to after commissioning, thereby reducing the utility's project financing costs. (Other regulated Southern states, including South Carolina and Georgia, have adopted similar pro-nuclear measures.) While some advocates challenged project costs during the course of the uprate projects, the commission generally approved the utility's cost requests. Elsewhere, a recent decision by the Georgia Public Service Commission demonstrated the discretion available to such bodies in traditionally regulated states: Georgia Power filed a request alongside its broader integrated resource investment plan to recover $175 million from customers in order to do early site evaluation work for a potential new nuclear plant in Stewart County. Following a commission staff report which recommended delaying a decision on the new plant, and testimony from advocates that the early evaluation cost be borne by the utility's investors rather than passed along to customers, the commission reduced Georgia Power's cost recovery authority to $99 million and required a status report to be filed before pursuing a 2019 project investment decision.[18]

---

18. Dave Williams, "Georgia Power Gets Green Light on New Nuclear Plant," *Atlanta Business Chronicle*, July 28, 2016.

States with Deregulated Environments

With the actions of traditionally regulated state public utility commissions more or less accepted as an understood baseline, the more relevant question might therefore be the options available to regulatory bodies in deregulated states. One approach here would be for commissions to require competitive electricity retailers or other load-serving entities in such states to enter into long-term power purchase agreements (PPAs) with existing independently owned nuclear power plants as part of their wholesale power supply portfolio, rolling the costs of doing so into the rates they charge end-use customers. This would be somewhat similar to recent developments in Ohio, where local distribution utilities owned by FirstEnergy, following a series of stakeholder compromises over an eighteen-month proposal period, in 2016 received approval from the Public Utilities Commission of Ohio to enter into an eight-year above-current-market-rate power purchase agreement with the nuclear power plant belonging to its competitive generation affiliate, FirstEnergy Solutions. That plant, Davis-Besse, had otherwise failed to clear recent PJM-territory energy auctions.[19] In this arrangement, the distribution utilities would pledge to purchase Davis-Besse generation over the period at a set price and then immediately resell that energy (along with associated capacity value and ancillary services) onto the daily and hourly PJM wholesale market. Utility end-use customer rates would reflect the difference between the agreed PPA and market price, whether higher or lower over time. (The expectation was that this would amount to extra costs in early years of the PPA and potentially lower prices later in the PPA if

---

19. The distribution utilities were Ohio Edison, the Illuminating Company, and Toledo Edison. FirstEnergy originally proposed fifteen-year PPAs, arguing that the longer length of time was needed to encourage plant investment. Regulatory Commission staff initially recommended rejection of FirstEnergy's proposal as being too expensive for customers and suggested that three-year PPAs might be more appropriate given market uncertainty in natural gas market conditions. The final proposal settled at eight years. Gavin Bade, "What's at stake in the FirstEnergy and AEP Ohio Power Plant Subsidy Hearings," *Utility Dive,* October 1, 2015.

rising natural gas prices were to increase PJM average power market prices.) FirstEnergy described the deal as a sort of consumer hedge that would also provide financial stability to a threatened nuclear plant, while rival natural gas-oriented utilities decried it as an unfair subsidy.[20] In this way, supporters argued that while the step would undeniably result in customers paying more for nuclear power today, it might save customers money—or not necessarily end up costing customers more—over time. Despite the state regulator's approval, however, the Federal Energy Regulatory Commission struck down the PPA deal before it could begin, arguing that the deal was anticompetitive given parent FirstEnergy's ownership interest in Davis-Besse.[21] It is possible that such an arrangement—with the distribution utility entering into a nuclear-specific PPA, even if above market—could nevertheless be attempted elsewhere with different circumstances, ownership or otherwise. Requiring above-market PPAs of distribution utilities for particular generation assets is a mainstay of utility-scale solar and wind development in competitive or semi-deregulated power markets (though such mechanisms are generally carried out "voluntarily" by distribution utilities with a generator of choice, albeit under a mandatory renewables portfolio standard or similar directive).

As this example illustrates, recent years have found regulatory commissions in deregulated, regional transmission market states more encumbered by FERC or FERC-related decisions. Though FERC's jurisdiction of the power system is limited to interstate wholesale markets, that lens has been applied in surprising ways to the efforts of individual states to direct the form of their own power system development. For

---

20. "FirstEnergy Ohio Utilities Announce Powering Ohio's Progress, a Long-Term Electric Rate Stability Plan," FirstEnergy, news release, August 4, 2014; Thomas Overton, "Fight Over Ohio Power Plant Subsidies Keeps Expanding," *Power* magazine, January 13, 2016.

21. Gavin Bade, "FERC Blocks Ohio Power Plant Subsidies for AEP and FirstEnergy," *Utility Dive*, April 28, 2016.

example, in a 2016 ruling, the US Supreme Court ruled that Maryland's proposed "contract for differences" approach to incentivizing new (in this case, nonnuclear) generation capacity by committing local distribution utilities to enter into twenty-year fixed PPAs, for later resale on the wholesale market, unlawfully infringed on FERC's jurisdiction of interstate electricity markets.[22] At the same time, the justices noted that their decision in this case does not address "the permissibility of various other measures States might employ to encourage development of new or clean generation, including tax incentives, land grants, direct subsidies, construction of state-owned generation facilities, or re-regulation of the energy sector." Despite these assurances, the experiences in Maryland and Ohio have made deregulated state commissions think more carefully about potential jurisdiction or other legal challenges to new incentive or subsidy programs.

New York's Approach

Utility commissions within deregulated states who wish to at least temporarily direct additional customer funds toward nuclear power may wish to model their efforts on existing mechanisms. For example, New York State was faced with the potential shutdown of three in-state nuclear plants for market performance reasons, with aggressive electricity sector carbon reduction goals to be met. The New York State executive and regulatory organs, including the governor's office, the cross-cutting New York State Energy Research and Development Authority, and the New York State Department of Public Service (the regulator), in 2016 proposed a nuclear zero-emission credit program to ensure that a minimum level of nuclear energy (or capacity) is maintained in the state.

---

22. CPV Maryland LLC vs Talen Energy Marketing, April 2016. FERC designated the PJM wholesale capacity auction as the sole rate-setting mechanism within that region; the state's efforts were thereby deemed to infringe on that mechanism.

This approach is nominally akin to that used to implement renewables portfolio standards, whereby each megawatt-hour of generation is awarded a transferrable renewable energy credit, of which distribution utilities are obligated to hold a certain number over time. Practically, however, the Department of Public Service later determined that given the market concentration of nuclear generators, it was not viable to establish a fair market price for the zero-emission credits that they would generate. Instead, the state's Energy Research & Development Authority was named as the sole buyer of credits at an initial administratively set price of $17.48 per megawatt-hour with a rising cap to as high as a nominal $29.15 per megawatt-hour over a twelve-year period. This agency would then resell the credits to obligated local distribution utilities or other designated load-serving entities in proportion to their share of total statewide electricity sales.[23] Meanwhile, if the regional wholesale electricity market price were to exceed a nominal $39 per megawatt-hour price over that period (up from a current average of about $30 per megawatt-hour), the subsidy would be adjusted down using a set formula.[24]

The design of New York's policy approach can therefore be regarded as a hybrid to meet at least two social goals, defined by the regulator as

---

23. The extra costs incurred would be passed on to the volumetric energy commodity charge in customer bills. Though the credits acquired would then be deemed un-tradable, it was left as an open possibility that load-serving entities could establish a similar but separate arrangement directly with a nuclear generating station so long as doing so would not shift costs onto other ratepayers.

24. While the stated goal of this production subsidy was to make the three existing plants economically viable in a competitive wholesale market, the level of the subsidy was calculated based on the federally determined global social cost of carbon ($42.87 per short ton in 2017 and rising with inflation) minus the expected price within the region's existing Regional Greenhouse Gas Initiative carbon dioxide emission trading market ($10.41 at its floor), to determine a net nominal carbon dioxide externality cost of $32.47. This was then translated into an initial $17.48 per nuclear megawatt-hour generation equivalent using the expected carbon intensity of a replacement fossil generation mix, were an existing nuclear plant to shut down (New York Public Service Commission 2016).

being in the public interest: (1) internalizing to the market the external value of nuclear's zero carbon emission generation[25] and (2) ensuring minimum market viability—but not windfall profits—for these three existing plants for their expected useful asset life, at the least cost.[26] Notably, since the program caps credit generation from each facility at its historical maximum annual generation level, the mechanism is not intended to support plant capacity increases or new construction. In short, the regulator described the policy as a pragmatic solution to a difficult issue, one that could be relatively swiftly implemented to meet market timelines without substantively disrupting the state's numerous other energy or environmental policies and regulations.[27]

Long-term PPAs
Encouraging long-term PPAs between distribution utilities and non-regulated generators, or otherwise mandating generation-specific subsidies, might sound a lot like re-creating a traditionally regulated operating environment within a purportedly deregulated framework. A more straightforward, if radical, approach for utility regulators wishing to direct more ratepayer funds toward nuclear power could therefore be to selectively re-regulate: place existing nuclear power plants (or aspects of those assets, such as new expansionary uprate investments) within a utility rate base to recover costs from captive customers. While such a step would likely have to be taken through legislation rather than utility

---

25. New York regulators described the emission challenge by pointing out that the shutdown of a single nuclear unit would wipe out the state's previous decade of gains made from wind power deployment and other low-carbon power generation incentive strategies.

26. Program participants include Nine Mile Point Nuclear Station units 1 and 2, James A. Fitzpatrick, and the R.E. Ginna Nuclear Power Plant. Indian Point units 2 and 3, which are the target of antinuclear activism in part due to their proximity to New York City, were not included in the initial program scope.

27. In fact, the Illinois legislature in late 2016 mimicked New York's retail-based approach in passing its own nuclear rescue bill, specifically designed to avoid falling foul of FERC wholesale market interference rules.

commission regulation, once authorized the regulator would then restart the traditional statewide integrated resource planning processes with the intent of supporting existing (or new) nuclear power. The dynamic effects of such a step could be widespread, however, potentially affecting a host of other power system modernization objectives, including price competition through new market entry, energy efficiency goals, distributed power generation, and smart grid deployment. At the same time, it would belie a power system regulatory environment which relies heavily on fledgling market structures to deliver reliable and affordable power while also increasingly leaning on the electricity system to meet growing social or environmental public policy goals through a variety of intervening mechanisms of varying elegance and efficacy. Evaluations of experiences with deregulation do suggest that the benefits of competitive markets have been only mixed in the first place (Borenstein and Bushnell 2015). No new state has begun a deregulation process since California's aborted experience following its 2001 electricity crisis. But there has been little public appetite to seriously consider re-regulation, even in a targeted capacity such as this.

Alternately, state regulatory commissions could reduce the amount that customers pay for renewables, arguing that their attributes (namely intermittency) incur external system costs.

Conversely, rather than paying more for nuclear power to improve its market viability, state regulatory commissions (or, in regional markets, regional transmission system operators) could instead reduce the amount that ratepayers pay for competitors to nuclear power, namely renewables. While states or regional system operators cannot control the existence of the current federal tax subsidies directed to renewables, they can influence electricity market rules.

For example, most electricity wholesale markets currently feature three main products: energy (both day-ahead and real-time), reserves (or ancillary services), and capacity. Energy is the obvious bulk commodity—a certain number of megawatt-hours at a certain time of day—and represents most of what a large baseload generator such as a nuclear power plant is paid. Ancillary service and reserves represent a generator's ability to offer power when called upon by the transmission operator to balance the grid in the short term. This is a major income source for standby natural gas peaking power plants, for example, and is also often won to some degree by nuclear generators, representing an income of a few dollars per megawatt-hour, depending on the region. Renewable energy generators generally do not win reserves payments because they are not dispatchable on demand. In effect, their presence on the grid helps create demand for reserve and ancillary products from other generators. Capacity markets are intended to incentivize the development of enough secure backup capability for different potential grid stress scenarios over the longer term (see further discussion on capacity markets below).

One current question is whether the energy and reserves wholesale market structure itself represents a form of subsidy to renewable power generators with unreliable output. An alternative would be to instead require that all generation that is bid into a wholesale market, or generation exceeding some threshold of variable resources, be reliably "firmed" with backup capacity to some standard. Doing this would essentially raise the marginal price at which renewable generators would be able to bid into the wholesale market (due to the likely need to pay other generators for balancing bilateral transactions), increasing wholesale clearing prices or otherwise reducing the amount of renewable generation clearing the market at a given price. It would make renewable generation—if provided without firming capacity—a less valuable resource. It would also help create a clearer signal in terms of the overall cost of firming these resources. Alternately, given that the presence of intermittent generation on a grid does incur costs elsewhere on the system, state regulators themselves could estimate this current "external" system-wide cost and assign a portion of it as a surcharge on renewables bid into the wholesale market. (These costs can occur directly through the need for backup firming capacity or, more indirectly, through complementary

subsidy schemes for intermittency-balancing investments in new transmission lines, grid storage, demand response, or other advanced distribution grid infrastructure.) These incremental costs are today socialized
across other generation sources or ratepayers directly.

Regarding point of application, were regional system operators to
decline to make these sorts of changes to wholesale interstate markets,
state regulatory agencies, even in regional markets, could potentially
apply similar mechanisms through their jurisdiction over distribution
utilities—requiring, for example, load-serving entities to demonstrate
and include the cost of energy firming within the long-term PPAs that
they currently sign with grid-scale renewables developments. One result
of this could be to make the costs of long-term PPAs from competing
nuclear generators relatively more attractive.

Of course, the same critique could be applied to such a mechanism as
the nuclear industry currently levels at subsidized renewables: though it
helps one form of generation, to the extent that it ends up displacing
other low- or zero-carbon technologies, no real environmental gains are
obtained. An alternative could therefore be to not focus on making
renewables less valuable on account of their intermittency, but rather
make conventional fossil capacity less valuable on account of its environmental externalities. Along these lines, this could take the form of either
a wholesale market price floor on fossil generation or a surcharge added
to fossil generation bid into the market representing its local or global
pollution characteristics. This would in essence be a power sector-specific
carbon tax through the back door.

State legislators could mandate certain levels of nuclear generation or they could direct taxpayer money to nuclear generators.

While many state regulatory commissions have considerable jurisdictional flexibility in their ability to affect the form of the power system,
they generally work within the confines of any relevant laws created by
state legislatures or, in some cases, the administrative policies of the
governor's office.

One common example of legislative engagement of state power issues in recent years has been the establishment of renewables portfolio standards. Through their mandates for load-serving entities to acquire certain types of zero-carbon power, these standards effectively increase the amount of ratepayer funds that are directed toward, for example, wind, solar, geothermal, or biomass power generators. This is usually done by compelling long-term power purchase agreements to be signed that otherwise would not be pursued (given their above-market prices), with penalties for noncompliance.

One straightforward option available to state legislators, of course, would be to simply mandate "nuclear portfolio standards" in the same vein as renewables portfolio standards, or otherwise create nuclear-specific carve-outs within an existing RPS, as is commonly done for solar, biogas, or other higher-cost alternative generation technologies (Bingaman et al. 2014). No state has successfully pursued such an effort. Alternately, a legislature could attempt to modify an existing renewables standard—or, perhaps more feasibly, modify a standard that is being extended or expanded—to instead be a technology-agnostic "low carbon portfolio standard" giving the compelled load-serving entity the flexibility to determine how to best meet the target. In addition to nuclear, such a standard could also count large hydropower, for example, another zero carbon baseload generation technology that is otherwise generally excluded from RPS policies.

On the one hand, such an approach is intellectually appealing, given a commonly understood expectation that renewables standards are ultimately justified based on the expectation that they will reduce a state's carbon emissions. When such laws were first being drafted over the past ten to fifteen years, there was little concern that nuclear power was threatened; in fact, many expected the US nuclear industry to dramatically expand in a new nuclear renaissance. So it is understandable that nuclear was excluded from these mechanisms.[28] Certainly it was not

---

28. Ohio is perhaps the only exception, whereby half of its 25 percent standard is eligible to be met by nuclear resources (existing nuclear represents just under half that quota in Ohio today). Implementation of the Ohio standard is currently frozen.

expected that increasingly aggressive renewables portfolio standards would end up, if not directly displacing existing zero carbon generation (as has been cited in the proposed closure of the Diablo Canyon Nuclear Power Plant in California[29]), then at least compromising nuclear power's market viability. The target was fossil generation.[30]

On the other hand, renewables portfolio standards as they stand, while costly (Sweeney 2008) and unfair to other low-emission technologies, have generally been both effective at meeting their specific deployment objectives (Barbose 2016) and reasonably politically popular (Bingaman et al. 2014). They have built up strong constituencies in the states which have them and they have shown resistance to modification, even during extensions which would have preserved or continued to grow renewables' share of sales. To paraphrase one influential state regulator, "The politics of tinkering with an RPS are just not worth it—renewables standards are about renewables, not carbon emissions."

---

29. To quote from PG&E's shutdown proposal documents: "After considering factors including, but not limited to, (i) the increase of the Renewable Portfolio Standard (RPS) to 50 percent by 2030 . . . PG&E in consultation with the Parties has concluded that the most effective and efficient path forward for achieving California's SB 350 policy goal for deep reductions of GHG emissions is to retire Diablo Canyon at the close of its current operating license period (PG&E 2016a)"; "Retirement of Diablo Canyon on the timeframe agreed to in the Joint Proposal will allow for increased flexibility for the California electric system so as to help maximize the value of solar and other variable resources that will be a crucial part of meeting PG&E's renewable targets and California's renewable and GHG emissions goals. Additionally, due to expected overgeneration throughout parts of the year, Diablo Canyon may contribute to higher system costs as its current generation profile causes challenges for efficiently integrating renewable resources. Therefore, if Diablo Canyon were not relicensed, the cost to integrate renewables could be lower (PG&E 2016b)."

30. For example, the preamble of Senate Bill 1078, California's first renewables portfolio standard, adopted in 2002, describes adopting the standard "for the purposes of increasing the diversity, reliability, public health and environmental benefits of the energy mix." The next paragraph goes on to state, "The development of renewable energy resources may ameliorate air quality problems throughout the state and improve public health by reducing the burning of fossil fuels and the associated environmental impacts." See California State Senate Bill No. 1078, Chapter 516.

Illustrating this, a coalition of California utilities in 2015 backed the concept of a low-carbon portfolio standard to replace and expand upon the state's existing 33 percent renewables standard. Instead, the legislature passed a simple enlargement of the renewables-only standard to 50 percent without significant public opposition.[31] In Illinois, a 2015 bill proposed by nuclear utilities to expand that state's renewables standard to become a low-carbon portfolio standard passed committee but failed to pass the broader legislature—practically, it would have added a $2 per month surcharge to customer bills to subsidize the state's existing nuclear plants. This approach had been one of five recommendations of the state's interagency working group, convened by the legislature to study the prospect of early nuclear closures in the state.[32] Utilities reintroduced a similar bill as a "zero emission standard" in 2016, but it was not voted on by the end of the gridlocked legislative session and Exelon subsequently announced the planned retirement of its Illinois Clinton (2017) and Quad Cities (2018) nuclear plants.[33]

In fact, rather than adopting a theoretically elegant technology-agnostic low-carbon portfolio standard, a special session of the Illinois legislature in December 2016 instead passed a broad package of statewide energy reforms dubbed the Future Energy Jobs Bill (SB 2814), which included significant aid for nuclear power plants. Underscoring the indistinct partisan lines of nuclear power, the process witnessed the ad hoc

---

31. In November 2016, PG&E CEO Tony Earley described the aborted effort, saying, "We fought to make it a 50 percent greenhouse-gas-free requirement, in which case Diablo [Canyon Nuclear Power Plant] would not have shut down." See Kahn, "Anti-nuclear movement."

32. Other options included relying upon "external forces and initiatives" undertaken by PJM/MISO or the EPA's proposed Clean Power Plan, a "sustainable power planning standard," a cap-and-trade program, or a carbon tax (Illinois Commerce Commission et al. 2015).

33. Exelon indicated it would continue to work with Illinois lawmakers on its so-called Next Generation Energy Plan subsidy bill before taking irreversible shutdown actions. See Gavin Bade, "Exelon to Shut Clinton, Quad Cities Nuclear Plants after Illinois Bill Stalls," *Utility Dive*, June 2, 2016.

back-and-forth formation and dissolution of political factions, variously including nuclear utilities, coal-fired power generator owners, renewables advocates, efficiency advocates, residential retail market reformists, and antinuclear activists. The bill saw thirty rounds of changes.[34] Ultimately, about $235 million annually of the bill's new subsidies and pass-through utility spending was approved for nuclear "zero-emission credits," analogous to the New York model, and about $600 million annually for efficiency and renewables.[35]

State legislators could make fossil fuel generation more expensive.

Alternately, and as with the regulatory commissions described above, state-level politicians or bureaucrats, through law or policy, could pursue options that would make nuclear power's competitors more expensive. For example, they could increase the stringency of existing carbon pricing programs such as the Regional Greenhouse Gas Initiative or California's AB 32 cap-and-trade program to raise their effective tax on fossil fuel generators. Note that New York is party to the Regional Greenhouse Gas Initiative, a power-sector carbon emission trading program, but one which due to permit oversupply has seen historic auction prices near its price floor of $2 per metric ton—substantially below federal estimates for the globally realized social cost of carbon,[36] as was later used in a bench-

---

34. Peter Maloney, "Illinois passes sweeping energy bill with support for Exelon nuclear plants," *Utility Dive*, December 2, 2016.

35. As in New York, Illinois's nuclear zero-emission credit program compels distribution utilities in the state to purchase 16 percent of their 2014 load in such credits for a period of ten years at a price equal to the grid's replacement social cost of carbon ($16.50 per megawatt-hour), escalating by $1 each year and subject to a baseline cost control valve. Illinois has a Democratic-controlled legislature and a Republican governor. Coal plant owners were ultimately excluded from the compromise broad legislative package and in return threatened lawsuits, arguing, as similarly contested in New York, that it interferes with FERC's control of wholesale power markets. Those cases are pending.

36. In 2016, the US Interagency Working Group (July 2015 revision) global social cost of carbon ranged from an approximate nominal $42.80 (at a 3 percent

mark for that state's zero-emission credit program. Permits in California's cap-and-trade program similarly sell at auction near their current $12.73 per ton (May 2016) price floor, which was not enough to justify keeping the San Onofre Nuclear Generating Station online when it encountered high repair costs and advocate opposition.[37] Were these programs to reduce the number of emission allocations to be auctioned or in circulation, they could potentially aid the economic value of nuclear power plants within their territories. Interested neighboring states with nuclear power plants could also opt-in to these existing programs (Washington State with its Columbia Nuclear Generating Station, for example, in the case of the AB 32 cap-and-trade program). Or they could establish their own broad-based carbon pricing systems (as is being explored with a potential revenue-neutral carbon tax in Oregon, which hosts the Trojan Nuclear Power Plant).

Grid operators: FERC, ISOs, and RTOs could reform electricity market rules, such that nuclear generation becomes more desirable in auctions.

As states moved to deregulate their electricity sectors in recent decades, the most basic step was to introduce competition into the wholesale

---

discount rate) to $64.20 (at a 2.5 percent discount rate) (EPA 2013). Note that this estimate includes worldwide expected damages from the emission of carbon dioxide in any one region. It has been argued that only the US share of those expected damages should be used in US rulemaking; doing so reduces this figure substantially, closer to the Regional Greenhouse Gas Initiatives and California AB 32 current market prices.

37. PG&E's testimony (2016b) on its proposal to close Diablo Canyon Nuclear Power Plant following its license expiration date cites potential high operating costs of $102 per megawatt-hour in 2025 as a barrier to the plant's viability, but notes that most of that cost escalation would be due to new state or federal regulatory costs, including potential (but not yet decided) multibillion-dollar mitigation costs to comply with once-through cooling regulations. In 2013, PG&E estimated its average production cost of the plant at $27.80 per megawatt-hour and noted that it was profitable (PG&E 2013). Economic viability can be said to be the primary driver of the (enacted and proposed) shutdowns of both California plants.

electrical generation market. Vertically integrated monopoly utilities were forced to unbundle their generation, transmission, and distribution assets; new investors were allowed to build independent power plants; and control of the transmission grid was handed over to an independent, generally nonprofit, entity, tasked to fairly and efficiently accept power generation from different providers through market bidding systems. As such, the characteristics of the power generation fleet would be market-driven, as opposed to being guided by state regulatory commission utility investment approval processes. The main goals in establishing these wholesale electricity markets were to reduce customer costs through efficiencies—both foreseen and unexpected—and to spread the profits of the power sector over more players.

It is important to note that while the ISOs and multistate RTOs that were granted control of these wholesale markets do remain responsible for ensuring system reliability, they were not formally charged with maintaining diversity or other particular characteristics among the generation fleet, as state regulatory commissions often did. And market design choices reflect that. Apart from some notable failures, such as California's electricity crisis in the early days of its deregulation effort, these markets have basically functioned well day-to-day and month-to-month. Their managers, in conjunction with the federal interstate transmission regulator FERC, periodically introduce conservative tweaks to market rules and designs to address various problems. But these markets are also all relatively young compared to the long investment lifetimes of power sector built infrastructure; nuclear's current challenges, in particular, contribute to the question of whether the markets are appropriately allocating electricity sector resources so as to meet a broader set of longer-term goals or if they should remain more narrowly focused on the short-term efficient operation of the grid.

The investor-owned utilities that operate in such markets are similarly incentivized to show quarterly profits rather than take on long-term, capital-intensive, and potentially individually risky infrastructure investments. Representatives of today's major nuclear utilities have noted that a pure fiduciary strategy might have led them to already retire the majority of their existing nuclear plants years ago, forcing them to lobby public shareholders on the value of hewing to a longer-term strategy or even assuming private financial costs for public goodwill benefit. This is unlikely to be a broadly tenable approach for other publicly traded firms. Given this, the prospect of such utilities investing in potential new nuclear plants without substantial changes in the market incentives they face quarter-to-quarter is remote. [38]

Industry and regulatory veterans have commented that when developing the original deregulated market structures, they never envisioned an operating environment where one fuel (such as natural gas prices today) would become so cheap for so long, allowing that form of generation to consistently beat out any alternative that was not otherwise mandated by out-of-market policy or regulations. Instead, it was assumed that multiple competing forms of power generation would be essentially comparable in cost competitiveness, with technology-specific attributes and operational efficiencies being the stronger determinants of the uptake of different forms of generation. These observers have noted that, especially given the unprecedented fuel price trends of recent years, competitive wholesale markets would never be able to deliver the diversity of power generation technologies that exists in portfolios across the United States today, a diversity which generally offers positive public externalities, particularly in times of crisis—financial, physical, or natural. Although there are numerous examples of policies that mandate a minimum share of the electricity mix come from a particular technology,

---

38. At a recent industry conference for new nuclear technology vendors, a major nuclear utility representative reminded the audience that natural gas continued to trade well under $3 per million BTU and that the daily staffing needs of a 300-megawatt combined-cycle natural gas power plant are only eight employees, compared to hundreds for nuclear units. He noted, "In real estate, the key is location, location, location; for utilities considering future [nuclear] deployment it is cost, cost, cost. . . . Safety is a must and non-negotiable, it is your ticket to get into the stadium: you have to be cost-competitive to play."

nowhere in the United States is there an explicit maximum share specified for one form of generation.[39] For their part, RTOs and ISOs have generally maintained the perspective that they are tasked to operate markets and enforce rules given to them, and it is not their place to change those markets to prefer any particular type or character of generation such as state commissions might have once done: in some ways, those represented the very sorts of (short-term) inefficiencies that the markets were tasked to cut through. At the same time, the emergence of this "regulatory gap" within the deregulated landscape of sometimes indistinct jurisdictional boundaries and competing priorities is creating tension among sector stakeholders. Considering this, the issues described below represent the sorts of options that could potentially be pursued at the ISO/RTO jurisdictional level were there a desire to benefit nuclear or nuclear-style generation. More broadly, similar tactics might be used to encourage generation portfolio diversity among other technologies as well.

Energy Price Caps and "Uplift" Charges

In a competitive wholesale market, power generators will enter bids into a day-ahead (most sales occur here) or hour-ahead market, indicating the lowest price per megawatt-hour that they are willing to accept from a buyer in order to sell energy. Each generator submits bids; they are automatically ranked by the market operator in terms of their asking price from low to high; and bids above a certain threshold are denied once the market's level of energy demand is met. This creates a market price that fluctuates throughout the day or by location depending on how much

---

39. Ironically, France, which relies on nuclear power for over three-quarters of all its electricity needs—the highest such share in the world—in 2015 adopted a cap on nuclear's maximum generation share and requires it to further fall to just 50 percent of the total by 2025. This was done partly in order to create addressable market share for new wind and solar power. A requirement of the construction of a new European Pressurized Reactor in the French village of Flamanville was to shut down an existing nuclear reactor at Fessenheim.

energy is expected to be needed by customers and how cheaply any number of generators are willing to offer it for. Generators more expensive than the cutoff price make no sale. In most markets, any generator submitting a bid less than the cutoff price makes the sale at the cutoff "clearing" price, not the original offer price.

As a basic business practice, a power plant operator can therefore be expected to put in bids that equal that plant's "short-run" marginal cost of operation: the cost incurred for generating that extra megawatt-hour of power versus remaining idle. If the market-clearing price ends up above the plant's marginal cost, the operator makes that much short-run profit. If the clearing is the same as the marginal cost, the operator is indifferent. Since nuclear power has a very low marginal cost of generation, operators will generally dispatch it with a zero price bid or, given the potential costs needed to temporarily idle the plant, they will even bid the plant as "must-run," meaning that they will continue generating power no matter what the market price is—even if negative. This ensures that, apart from refueling periods, maintenance, or other downtime, a nuclear plant runs 24/7, receiving whatever the market-clearing price is for that generation. Its overall revenues are therefore largely beholden to the market around it.

One way nuclear operators can make substantial profits is by selling energy when the market price spikes—for example, when demand is otherwise high, such as in the early evening on a hot day, and supply is constricted. Such price spikes routinely occur and are generally temporary in nature, with the high market prices providing an incentive for additional supply to come online—an old or inefficient gas-fired power plant, for example—or for customer demand to weaken. Given the fear during deregulation, however, that freewheeling markets could naturally or through manipulation result in politically untenable price spikes that ultimately drive up consumer bills (given that most consumers are unable to observe or respond to real-time prices), many markets instituted price caps which limit just how high a megawatt-hour of energy can be sold during a spike. FERC once limited normal energy offer prices to $1,000 per megawatt-hour, for example. ISOs and RTOs since 2008 are able to set their own administrative offer price caps alongside other shortage pricing mechanisms meant to compensate operators for providing generation and reserves during tight market conditions. Since nuclear operators dispatch no matter the price, any time the price of energy is capped represents a lost profit opportunity. Removing or effectively raising any such administrative price caps could therefore improve the economics of existing nuclear power; doing so would require analyzing the potential impact on customers and should ideally be pursued in situations where new technologies, businesses, or market designs allow customers to effectively observe price spikes and moderate their demand in response.

A more obscure but related market design tweak for nuclear's benefit could be the way in which so-called uplift credits are currently handled. Since today's wholesale markets are not perfectly elegant modeled systems, a number of administrative or other mechanisms have been established to intervene in or supplement the market in order to keep the lights on and the generators paid. In the parlance of system operators, "consumers place a very high value on avoiding involuntary curtailments (FERC 2014b)." One result of this is the existence of uplift credits paid retroactively to generators by an ISO or RTO to make them whole for various operational edge cases. For example, a generator will generally bid its marginal production cost into the wholesale market in order to be scheduled for dispatch by the grid operator. But it may also incur costs during plant start-up or spin-down when it is not earning generation revenues. ISOs or RTOs therefore allow generators to retroactively bill for some of these costs, which will be especially notable for generators such as gas "peaker" plants, which often ramp up and down but have few generating hours during which to recover those extra start-up costs. Another example is for inflexible generators with long minimum run times (coal, for example), which an operator may wish to dispatch for one time period; later, the operator may no longer need that plant's energy or ancillary services to meet market needs, but the generator may need to still physically operate despite it being uneconomical to do so. Rather than allowing that inflexible (and potentially costly) generator to set the market-clearing price, however, grid operators will instead generally set the market price lower, at the level of a less expensive resource which is withdrawn from the market in order to make room for the inflexible generator. The result is an uplift payment made to the inflexible generator to compensate it for having to operate through an uneconomical period.

According to FERC, total uplift credits to generators (which are ultimately passed through to customers through uplift charges) average just over $1 billion per year nationwide, or a range from $0.30 to $1.40 per megawatt-hour. This is relatively small when compared to overall energy costs, but the payments tend to be concentrated both regionally and temporally, at times exceeding $10 per megawatt-hour at some locations and with a few individual plants receiving tens of millions of dollars in credits annually.[40] While the dynamics are complex, uplift charges are of interest to the existing nuclear situation because they tend to suppress wholesale energy prices: rather than every bid reflecting the true cost of providing that power, some market bids are instead argued to effectively be artificially low, with the difference later backfilled in non-transparent make-whole payments. For nuclear, which generally dispatches all day, every day, suppressed wholesale energy prices mean lower revenues. Uplift credits are like the residual error term in an engineering model— the stubbornly inelegant affirmations of reality. Continuing to reform them so that more of the true costs of providing energy services is reflected in day-ahead or real-time market prices would include both administrative choices and the quality and accuracy of a grid operator's forecasting and management models.

For its part, FERC has recognized that "price formation" is not perfect in today's wholesale electricity markets: it started an investigation into a number of issues in 2014 through staff workshops, reports, and comment periods. In June 2016, it issued a final rule (Order 825) on settlement intervals and shortage pricing that could provide a model for ISO and RTOs to address some of the issues described above (FERC 2016).

---

40. For more on uplift charges and trends, see FERC (2014a).

Capacity Pricing Terms and Availability Incentives

As described above, wholesale energy markets provide two main products to a dispatching ISO or RTO: (1) the energy bulk commodity and (2) various forms of reserves, for which a generator stands by to offer power when called upon by the transmission operator to balance the grid day-to-day and month-to-month. (Examples are "regulation," "spinning," and "non-spinning"; the grid operator will direct certain generators to operate in different ways, as technically feasible, to maintain stability and will compensate those generators for the opportunity cost in doing so.) A large baseload generator will typically receive the bulk of its revenues from the energy market. In addition, many, but not all, ISOs and RTOs operate a separate longer-term "capacity" market. Capacity markets are add-ons to the main energy market and are intended to provide an additional economic signal for plant investors and operators to build additional infrastructure (capacity) within a grid's operating area over the medium to long term. In theory, an energy-only market *may* be able to provide enough incentive for investors to build new plants, simply through the price that they would eventually receive when generating. But the potential for rare events or unforeseen grid developments means that the additional capacity mechanism can nonetheless play a useful insurance role.

In capacity markets, the grid operator operates an auction to encourage enough new capacity development to meet established reliability margins (usually around 15–20 percent above expected future peak power demands). Alternately, capacity can also be delivered through demand response that reduces overall demand. There are a few ways to demonstrate or sell capacity. In PJM, for example, "megawatt-day" capacity responsibilities are auctioned for deliveries three years in advance: the lead time is intended to send a price signal to power plant operators and investors so that they can add new marginal uprate capacity to existing plants or even build new plants based on the grid operator's future reliability expectations. MISO currently operates year-ahead capacity auctions, but is considering switching to three-year-ahead markets.

Capacity prices in multistate RTOs are volatile both year-to-year and geographically across jurisdictions. This year's PJM results auction for 2019/2020 ranged from $100-$203 per megawatt-day for "capacity performance" products, for example, which are required to be available for sustained duty throughout the entire year.[41]

Though small in absolute terms, capacity payments are nonetheless an important component of nuclear plant business models. The "capacity performance" year-round-type product categories enacted in PJM and the New England ISO are thought to benefit nonseasonal baseload generators such as nuclear. A large nuclear power plant receiving capacity payments could expect additional revenues of tens of millions of dollars annually, depending on the clearing price. But capacity markets are not a panacea for nuclear. For example, Exelon reported that of its plants, two in the PJM service territory—Quad Cities and the single-unit Three Mile Island nuclear generating station in Pennsylvania—bid too high and did not pass 2016's capacity auction. Its Byron Generating Station in Illinois only partially cleared, while its single-unit Oyster Creek plant in New Jersey did not bid due to planned closure. Each of these stations has periodically failed capacity auctions in recent years. Six other Exelon PJM nuclear plants passed.

Capacity markets are not just meant as financial lifelines to existing power plants; in deregulated electricity markets that lack state regulatory commission-led integrated resource planning processes to guide new investments, they are also supposed to encourage new mechanisms or

41. Conventional "base capacity" products, which are focused on the summer months, traded at $20 per megawatt-day below that. Together, this resulted in 5.5 pledged gigawatts of new generation or uprate capacity, 3.9 gigawatts of out-of-RTO imports, 10.4 gigawatts of demand response, and 1.5 gigawatts of energy efficiency. Clearing prices were about 39 percent lower than last year's PJM forward auction and 17 percent lower than the year before that (in part due to the growing availability of cheap natural gas peaker plants as well as energy efficiency and demand response capacity products), but 68 percent higher than the 2013 auctions (PJM 2016a).

infrastructure to be built within the region to meet expected future reliability needs. In that regard, the impact on nuclear has been mixed at best. Returning to the PJM territory, where nineteen nuclear plants currently generate 32 percent of the total electricity supply, thirteen years of capacity auctions have incentivized the development of 46.2 total gigawatts of new generation capacity. But only 1.4 gigawatts of that has come from nuclear power—all from uprates to existing plants, none from new builds, and with no incremental capacity additions in the latest auction.[42] Natural gas provides 36.7 gigawatts. Market authorities argue that this is an efficient market outcome given the lower investment risk to building a natural gas combined-cycle or peaker plant compared to alternatives, with the savings passed on to customers. Nuclear advocates argue that the short lead times and terms of the market design—single-year products, just three years out (or shorter in the case of MISO)—systematically prefer the development of smaller gas plants over larger-scale and longer-term projects. Changing these two parameters—bidding out twenty-year capacity contracts, for example, with a five-year or longer lead time—could potentially help encourage new nuclear investment, at the expense of increased forecasting uncertainty around market needs further than three years into the future. Whatever the case, it is clear that the current diversity and form of the overall PJM generating fleet, itself largely the product of deliberate planning under regulated power markets, would not be achieved through the current capacity auction mechanisms (at least not given current fuel market conditions).

Address Renewables Impacts on RTO/ISO Energy Market Price Setting

The emergence of renewable generation such as wind and solar photovoltaics has affected wholesale energy markets in two ways that potentially hurt the profitability of nuclear power: (1) through federal deployment incentives, namely tax subsidies, and (2) through the mainstreaming of generation intermittency.

---

42. Covering capacity delivery terms from 2007/08 to 2019/20. See PJM 2016a (#5154776), 24.

As described earlier, the federal investment tax credit for solar and the production tax credit for wind may allow them to be profitable even when revenues from energy sales are less than averaged operating costs. The current $23 per megawatt-hour wind production tax credit in particular introduces the opportunity for some generators to produce revenues even while selling their generation at negative prices.[43] Nuclear generators claim that this has resulted in price suppression across a typical day's wholesale energy clearing prices, even leading to negative nighttime rates in some cases (Huntowski, Patterson, and Schnitzer 2012).[44] In response to these criticisms, the American Wind Energy Association, the industry's lobby and trade group, commissioned a study to argue that the PTC in itself does not substantively contribute to negative prices—wind bids are generally kept to about $0 per megawatt-hour, reflecting their natural near-zero marginal cost of generation—and that transmission constraints were a more important factor in negative pricing (Goggin 2014). Individual FERC commissioners have since weighed in on both sides of the issue.[45] The existence of negative prices, which would otherwise beg belief, suggests that the nuclear industry's complaints have merit.

Could negative bids be limited through regulation of RTOs? PJM first applied a so-called minimum offer price rule to its capacity market auctions in 2006 following concerns that some generators, who through other business arms may also be major buyers of power, could effectively

---

43. The wind PTC is said to account for about half of total revenues for many generators (*RTO Insider*, "Who's to Blame for Negative Prices?").

44. Exelon has claimed that competition from wind energy suppressed wholesale prices in northern Illinois, home to its Quad Cities Generating Station, by $6 per megawatt-hour over the period 2009–2013.

45. Hannah Northey, "FERC Debates Impact of Wind PTC, Transmission on Nuclear Fleet," *E&E News*, May 16, 2014. A Congressional Research Service monograph published in November 2012 found some evidence that wind generators benefiting from a PTC could distort wholesale energy markets but argued that this could be somewhat offset by the results of capacity markets or the common use of bilateral power purchasing agreements to hedge against volatility (Brown 2012).

game the market by submitting artificially low, uneconomical auction bids. In the years since, FERC has intervened in the details of such minimum offer price rules, at times requiring exemptions based upon generation type (state-supported renewables being exempted in PJM) or generator intent (exempting nuclear and hydropower generators, who would conceivably have no potential financial gain from suppressing prices) or even attempting to derive individual plant economics to determine the legitimacy of offers. But FERC has been fairly inconsistent in issuing such limitations over time and place: in the New England ISO, for example, renewables are not exempted as they are in PJM (Patterson and Reiter 2016).

Considering the larger picture, federal taxpayer-funded subsidies to renewables operators in the electricity market can be expected to lower prices from a no-subsidy alternative, especially in the case where a certain quantity of the subsidized generation is already required to be built by state renewables portfolio standards.[46] To the extent overall electricity prices are lowered as a result, electricity consumers recover some of their initial losses in funding the tax subsidy (including some redistribution of losses and benefits across different populations). Meanwhile, suppressed market pricing penalizes nonsubsidized competing electricity suppliers. In the end, the PTC in competitive markets could somewhat unexpectedly be seen as a mechanism to transfer profitability from nonsubsidized generators to subsidized generators. How important this is, and to what extent additional compensatory mechanisms should be developed to address it (barring repeal of the PTC itself), therefore depends on the share of any total market taken by federally subsidized renewables. Basically, it matters more when there is more wind (or solar) deployment.

---

46. Of course, policy is not made in a vacuum. The existence of the federal subsidy could in turn be argued to affect the political economy of a state's decision to pursue a renewables portfolio standard in the first place, just as state policymakers might otherwise consider industry's ability to meet the standard and associated overall costs.

Apart from the federal subsidy, the second novel impact of increased deployment of renewables is the way in which markets have adjusted, or will have to adjust, to accommodate for their combined intermittent and zero marginal cost nature. When the resource is available, it is able to generate revenues to the maximum extent that it can produce, but generally does not set the marginal price. When the resource is unavailable, it does not generate revenues or penalties. Instead, other resources are indirectly compensated to fill in the gap: renewables are not price-responsive. Generators of this type are able to exist within today's wholesale markets, but they are not well matched: consider the hypothetical case of a wholesale market populated entirely by intermittent, zero-marginal-cost renewables, which would fail to set a clearing price yet clearly still have significant system costs to be compensated. Even before that end-state, it is easy to imagine how a high-renewables-penetration electricity market would have clearing prices that fall toward zero during times of natural resource availability and that spike exactly when those renewables drop off due to lack of natural resources. This would fail to properly compensate the renewable resource. A near-zero marginal cost generation world, under current or proposed retail pricing models, would also fail to send useful real-time pricing information to guide demand response or even broader energy efficiency efforts, despite the continued system value in such demand-side efforts. Are there then potential alternative wholesale market designs better suited to accommodating renewables while reflecting generation costs for a variety of technologies, both capital-intensive and not?[47]

One proposal that goes beyond tweaking existing capacity markets, as described above, would be for RTOs to establish a new class of capacity auctions specifically for longer-term, low-carbon resources. This would effectively introduce a capital investment-based compensation model in parallel to the current generation revenue-based compensation model. It could be open to any low-carbon technology, including nuclear, but

---

47. See Keay (2016) for the genesis of and further discussion on many of the concepts described below, within the context of European energy markets.

would be designed with a longer investment timeframe so as not to de facto exclude nuclear or other potential long-lead-time low-carbon resources such as thermal plants with carbon capture and storage, solar thermal, geothermal, or new hydro. This could be done at the behest of, or in cooperation with, interested states, and any additional costs apportioned among that state's ratepayers, such that the impact on wholesale prices for nonparticipants would be unaffected and less likely to draw legal challenge. This could be seen as an alternative or even a complement to the current RPS model, with the potential political feasibility benefit of not needing to modify these otherwise generally supported, if expensive, policies. The key difference here is that once these zero- or low-marginal-cost resources were built, they would not then participate directly in a generation-based revenue market, reducing distortion on price-setting in that area. Costs for this could be passed on to the retail market in a variety of ways, but it could make sense to do so through separate flat, averaged, or peak demand charges on customer bills, rather than volumetric consumption-based rates.

Though there does not appear to be a precedent for such a model for supply-side resources, one could look at existing utility-led energy efficiency investments as a form of demand-side, capital-intensive, zero-marginal-cost resource development. As in the proposed model, energy efficiency investments are not currently bid into wholesale energy markets to cover costs—they are simply "dispatched" as available with all costs covered through an up-front capital investment remuneration scheme rather than through dispatch-based revenue compensation. Likewise, on the retail side, this often shows up as a separate fixed pass-through bill item, such as a "public goods charge" or "energy efficiency charge." It would make sense that a zero-carbon supply-side resource could fit within the same framework, distinguishable only by the additional share of capital costs incurred through their use of the transmission and distribution grid.

Another alternative model would be to create parallel markets for as-available, intermittent, dispatchable, and baseload generation sources (or firmed versus non-firmed resources). Each would have separate wholesale clearing prices, thereby reducing cross-technology price distortions. Intermediaries or end consumers could then choose to purchase firmed supplies, presumably at a premium price, or to purchase intermittent supplies presumably at a discount. For the intermittent supplies, the consumer or intermediary would then have to choose how to respond to the as-available nature: through voluntary or involuntary demand response, through additional capital investments in storage or distributed generation, or through contract-based hedging. In fact, this final option in many ways echoes the way that renewable power is often effectively sold today, through bilateral off-take contracts (with a guarantee to buy future production) where one party (generally the reseller) assumes the risk of intermittency. One key difference is that whereas the costs of this hedging today are essentially socialized across the broader system, under parallel markets they would be separated so as to reduce system-wide interaction effects on both the wholesale and, potentially, retail sides. Over time, costs for each market should converge toward the value of each resource (which itself could be dynamic, based on technology costs, transmission and distribution infrastructure availability, and overall generation portfolio mixes). This has the added value of sustainably supporting the scaled deployment of new grid technologies and other resources throughout the system.

Both of the above alternatives get at the idea that electricity markets should be flexible enough to best reflect, and expose, the attributes of its participants—here, capital intensiveness or dispatchability. A related but extended concept would be to carry this to its extreme by fully decentralizing electricity markets such that wholesale and retail markets are effectively merged, with a centralized or even a decentralized system manager. A so-called transactive pricing framework, for example, would take advantage of real-time communication between generators and consumers so that end-use customers could direct their energy trades in detail, in real time, and in response to dynamic changes across the grid—from the nature of the generation demanded and its reliability, to transmission or distribution capacity and constraints, and any dynamic response. Of course, in practice, a consumer would be likely to purchase packages of energy services and attributes through a bundler to both reduce transaction costs and hedge risks—with choices akin to the mobile phone subscriptions of today. The key characteristic of moving in this direction, however, would be to recognize that electricity is not a simple bulk commodity, but increasingly something with recognizable performance, economic, environmental, or even values-based attributes. Today, society largely relies on policies and regulations or other intermediary preferences to determine how to best encourage or allocate those attributes and values within a heavily confined market framework, and tensions arise when the results cannot satisfy heterogeneous preferences. Over time, a more transparent, dynamic, and customer-exposed energy market design could help move away from the political debates of "picking winners and losers."

Federal Agencies: The EPA could pursue environmental regulations that encourage the use of nuclear power at the state level.

In many ways, EPA regulatory actions under conventional local and regional air quality mandates of the Clean Air Act have been a boost to existing nuclear power plants. Recently enacted or announced regulations include the nitrogen- and sulfur dioxide-focused Cross-State Air Pollution Rule, updated National Ambient Air Quality Standards concerning fine particulate matter and ozone, and the Mercury and Air Toxics Standards. All attempt to address the "un-costed" environmental and human health impacts of coal-fired power generation and have in turn hurt the market viability of baseload coal-fired power generation, which competes with nuclear's own large-scale baseload generation in many markets.[48] The Associated Press in 2011 estimated that these com-

---

48. Members of the incoming Donald Trump administration have signaled their opposition to aspects of these rules or their overall effect on the US coal industry. While the new administration may therefore choose to deprioritize enforcement of these rules, or attempt other revisions that might loosen the standards, the

bined regulations would result in the closure of thirty-two coal plants in the short term, with another thirty-six at risk, mainly in the Midwest and East, representing about 8 percent of the fleet. Actual coal generation losses since then, in combination with extended and unexpectedly low natural gas prices, have exceeded those estimates: total US coal generation fell from 1.847 terawatt-hours in 2010 (44.8 percent of all power generation) to just 1.356 terawatt-hours in 2015 (33.1 percent).[49]

EPA actions under the Clean Water Act have been more mixed for nuclear. For example, EPA's Clean Water Act 316(b) rule on power plant cooling water intakes was issued in 1999 but has been in the courts ever since. A 2014 final rule dealt with the impacts of existing power plants' use of once-through cooling on aquatic life and affected over five hundred facilities nationwide; specific implementation was largely left to state regulatory agencies. In some states, such as California, this has led to the closure of a number of existing once-through-cooled gas-fired power plants, but has also resulted in both higher operating costs (through the payment of mitigation fees) for nuclear power and the possibility that plants could face closure due to the massive capital investment needed for compliance.[50]

---

overall body of regulations is likely to have significant inertia. Third-party advocates have engaged in effective "sue-then-settle" legal campaigns with the EPA in recent years to force regulation adoption. Also, coal plant owners faced with regulatory uncertainty may resist substantively revising long-term plans absent a dramatic change in the overall EPA air pollution regulatory framework or the emergence of game-changing new emissions technologies.

49. The vast majority of this decline has, however, been filled by new natural gas-fired as opposed to nuclear generation. It is worth noting, however, that coal plants—unlike nuclear—are in many cases able to effectively "mothball" plants to be later brought back online when operating conditions change.

50. A report commissioned by California's Review Committee for Nuclear Fueled Power Plants, for example, estimated the cost of various technical compliance options for the Diablo Canyon Power Plant: $8.6 billion to $14.1 billion for new freshwater wet or dry cooled cooling towers; $6.2 billion to $8 billion for saltwater cooling towers; and $456 million to $675 million for fish entrainment screening technology options; plus another $600 million to $700 million per year for

The EPA and Carbon

Going forward, a powerful new regulatory authority available to the EPA under the 2007 *Massachusetts vs. EPA* Supreme Court ruling is the mitigation of carbon dioxide emissions. The question is what tools EPA might deploy in its name. While that case focused on mobile sources such as automobiles, recent proposed or adopted EPA regulations have addressed stationary sources as well, including power plants. The agency's 2015 Clean Air Act Section 111(b) Carbon Pollution Standard for New Power Plants, for example, established New Source Performance Standards of 1,000 pounds of carbon dioxide emissions or less per megawatt-hour of electricity production from new natural gas power plants and 1,400 pounds of carbon dioxide emissions or less per megawatt-hour from new coal power plants. This effectively prohibited the construction of new conventional coal plants without carbon capture technologies, removing a major pillar of the American power generation technology mix from potential future competition with nuclear power.

More directly relevant to today's nuclear plants was the Obama administration EPA's proposed, but fiercely contested, Clean Air Act 111(d) Clean Power Plan, which aimed to regulate the carbon dioxide emissions of existing power plants by setting state-specific total (a.k.a "mass-based") or per megawatt-hour "rate-based" targets for the power generation fleet.[51] Its goals and basic form provided a useful window on

---

replacement power shutdown costs during construction (Bechtel 2014). The issues attracted significant attention from state environmental advocacy groups and regulatory agencies. See California Energy Commission, California Public Utilities Commission, the Center for Energy Efficiency and Renewable Technologies, and the Alliance for Nuclear Responsibility, "Subcommittee Comments on Bechtel's Assessment of Alternatives to Once-Through-Cooling for Diablo Canyon Power Plant," November 28, 2014, www.swrcb.ca.gov/water_issues/programs/ocean/cwa316/rcnfpp/docs/subbechcom_111314.pdf. The threat of these additional costs likely factored into the later proposal to shutter the plant at the end of its original operating license period.

51. The future of the Clean Power Plan, championed by the Obama administration's EPA, was brought into question following the November 2016 election of Donald Trump, who pledged to repeal the regulation.

potential federal regulatory strategies that might resurface under different political conditions, and how the nuclear industry might be better prepared to benefit from them. It is also worth noting that some states, having already prepared compliance plans for the regulation, may choose to implement elements of that framework voluntarily. The proposed plan initially met with criticism from the nuclear industry, but it gained more support following public comment-driven revisions. In sum, the Clean Power Plan as proposed by the Obama administration would likely have benefitted existing nuclear power versus fossil-fueled power plants, but not versus renewables.[52] Here is how:

The Clean Power Plan proposed a federalized implementation approach, something that might be carried over into any successor policy given the element of local flexibility it affords. Specifically, EPA directed states to choose one of two implementation program formats: emission mass-based or emission rate-based. The "mass-based" approach allowed the state to sum up all of its power sector emissions and then develop mechanisms to control the total emission amount, regardless of the future quantity of power generation. For example, a mass-based state could elect to develop a single state or even regional cap-and-trade program. This would allow a variety of generators (including some carbon-intensive coal generators) to continue operating in the state as long as the state made counter-balancing reductions elsewhere within the sector. For existing nuclear generators, this could be an appealing option if

---

52. Modeling undertaken in February 2016 by the Rhodium Group of the impact of (1) an extension of the federal solar and wind ITC and PTC and (2) the implementation of the EPA's Clean Power Plan found that there were important interaction effects among the two policies. Specifically, given tax extenders (as approved by Congress in late 2015) alone, nuclear power nationwide through 2030 would decline relative to the DOE's 2015 Annual Energy Outlook base case, as would natural gas, while wind and solar power would substantively gain. Adding the Clean Power Plan and tax extenders, wind and solar power would gain even more, but nuclear's losses would be somewhat mitigated versus the tax-extender-only case, with coal emerging as a major loser. In contrast, the Clean Power Plan alone would have benefited primarily natural gas, with some additional benefit to wind, solar, and nuclear versus the status quo.

states elected to freely allocate emission permits to existing generators based upon their current electricity output: as nuclear operators would not need the permits to cover their carbon-free generation, they could then sell these permits to fossil-fueled generators and book the revenue. Alternately, were a state to auction its emission permits directly, it might choose (but would not be obligated) to direct some of the revenue raised to support existing nuclear, as allowed by FERC market rules.

Under a "rate-based" approach, each power plant was instead to be assigned a technology-specific emissions rate limit, met on a plant-by-plant basis. Plants not able to meet their standard would acquire tradable emission rate credits from other parties or through emission-reducing investments undertaken elsewhere.[53] A rate-based plan would allow state power sector emissions to rise alongside growing power consumption, as long as emission rates were met.

In either case, new nuclear construction or uprates at existing plants would stand to benefit. In mass-based states, they could potentially be granted new tradable emission permits from the state that could be sold for revenue, or at least be exempt from having to purchase emission permits as a fossil-fuel plant would. In rate-based states, meanwhile, new capacity could potentially earn tradable emission rate credits to be sold to carbon-emitting generators. New renewable generation would receive essentially identical benefits to nuclear. The value of such benefits to nuclear, under the Clean Power Plan or any similar regulation, would depend on the stringency of a state's emission reduction target, the type of market chosen, cross-state trading options, and the relative costs for other potential forms of low-carbon power generation or energy efficiency. In a 2016 study, the PJM Interconnection estimated that new nuclear (or other zero carbon) sources under a rate-based market could expect to receive additional "out of market" revenues of $14 per megawatt-hour from the credits earned during operations (PJM 2016b). Under mass-based markets, where there are not additional direct payments (unless allocated by the state), new nuclear units would expect to see an

---

53. Alternately, states could fulfill a state-specific emission rate limit.

additional $1.70 in revenue per megawatt-hour of generation simply from the higher overall energy market prices that carbon dioxide emission regulations would induce.[54]

Surprisingly for a policy intended to reward low-carbon power plants, however, the benefits to existing nuclear power from EPA's plan would have been mixed at best. While PJM estimated that the total net present value of emission markets across its territory under the plan through 2030 could have ranged from $6.91 billion to $13.46 billion, nuclear would have only been able to capture a minority share of that. For example, the final proposed rule would not have provided direct benefit to nuclear license extensions: a rate-based pathway would not have allowed investments in license extension (often hundreds of millions of dollars) to generate new emission rate credits. This led to criticism from the nuclear industry that the Obama Administration's EPA took continued operation of the existing nuclear fleet for granted. Moreover, other aspects of the plan flatly preferred renewables over nuclear, without providing justification. The plan's proposed Clean Energy Incentive Program, a sub-section akin to a corporate gift-matching program for states that undertake early emission reductions, was not technology-neutral: any new investments in renewables (wind, solar, geothermal, or hydropower generation) undertaken at the beginning of the program would have doubled the emission rate credits they generate from a matching pool provided by the EPA, making those particular projects more financially attractive and the state's overall targets easier to meet in the long run. Another sub-section, the renewable energy set-aside, created a 5 percent allowance pool in mass-based states for only renewables, purportedly in order to avoid emission leakage. Meanwhile, the

---

54. Practically, however, new nuclear units were unlikely to be significantly helped by this version of the Clean Power Plan, which set states' compliance targets for the year 2030 (likely too short a period to go through a regulatory compliance, construction, and commissioning phase for a new-build plant), unless there were some regulatory certainty that emission regulations would extend beyond that timeframe. In PJM's own modeling, for example, it did not expect the construction of any new nuclear power plants from the introduction of EPA regulations.

plan's proposed output-based allocation reserve specifically rewarded existing natural gas combined-cycle power plants for increasing their generation output from historical levels. Here again, nuclear was excluded.

Given the unlikely future of the proposed Clean Power Plan itself under the Trump administration's EPA, it may be more pertinent to consider the general implications of future EPA "stationary-source" greenhouse gas regulations that would affect existing power plants. Were EPA to take any actions that increase the cost of doing business for currently operating fossil-fuel facilities, this would result in at least short-term wholesale electricity price increases. In such a situation, nuclear power would stand to benefit (in an absolute sense, if not relative to other clean energy technologies) from additional energy or capacity market revenues given its operating mode as a price-taker in most competitive markets. Again returning to PJM's regional modeling as one example, existing nuclear plants in that service area were expected to become marginally more profitable through 2030 given EPA's previously-proposed carbon dioxide regulatory restrictions, with average plant revenues improving from $1 to $2 per megawatt-hour by 2030 compared to the reference case, depending on the form of the market.

Another issue to consider is that any benefits to nuclear power from potential power sector carbon dioxide emission reduction rules would directly scale alongside the stringency of the targets. Many states expressed their clear opposition to the Obama EPA rules, citing the new compliance costs it would incur or special regional impacts. But some environmental advocates argued that the plan at a national level was actually too lenient.[55] Of course, once the framework is set, one would expect that any overall or state-level carbon dioxide targets might be

---

55. A 2015 analysis by Michael Wara and co-authors at Stanford University, for example, argued that the Clean Power Plan's targets may not have even been binding on emissions overall given that the natural growth rate in nationwide electricity consumption may have been slower than expected by the policy (Wara, Cullenward, and Teitelbaum 2015).

adjusted downward over time to become more stringent. "Ratcheting" is common in target-based environmental regulations—state-level RPS programs, for example.[56]

Are there other steps that the EPA might take to fulfill its apparent obligations to regulate carbon dioxide emissions that could affect nuclear? The Clean Power Plan relied on a radical expansion of a previously minor statue of the Clean Air Act (the authority from Congress under which EPA carries out many of its air pollution regulatory actions) for its legal basis.[57] New EPA actions might instead look to further direction from Congress rather than relying on purely administrative actions. Given that, costs of regulation will be a major consideration: the EPA, for example, might try to encourage nuclear generation directly without necessarily increasing the costs of gas- and coal-fired competitors in the process. To speculate, proposed nuclear shutdowns might trigger requirements around the carbon-intensity of replacement power. Alternately, new investments in the maintenance, refurbishment, license extension, or power uprate of existing plants or plant fuel cycles could gain preferential treatment along the lines of best available emission control technologies. Such capabilities are well-established, unlike some of the more experimental greenhouse gas emission reduction efforts that EPA has suggested be implemented for other power generation technologies, such as carbon-capture. Both approaches would recognize the reality that many existing zero-carbon nuclear plants face pressures to shut down or otherwise limit future operations in the current market environment.

---

56. Of the 29 RPS states, about half have increased their targets or added on new requirements since original adoption—multiple times in some instances. In contrast, only two states have weakened RPS targets, despite a number of legislative proposals to do so.

57. The Clean Air Act section 111 part d states: ". . . each State shall submit to the Administrator a plan which (A) establishes standards of performance for any existing source for any air pollutant (i) for which air quality criteria have not been issued . . . but (ii) to which a standard of performance under this section would apply if such existing source were a new source . . ."

Other Federal Climate Regulatory Tools

Other EPA regulatory actions to address greenhouse gas emissions could also raise the costs of nuclear's fossil-fueled competitors. The Obama administration, for example, set a goal of reducing US methane emissions by 45 percent from 2012 levels by 2045; the EPA in May 2016 released a final rule concerning methane leaks from new and modified sources, including upstream oil and gas wells as well as gas processing, transmission, and distribution infrastructure. This was the agency's first direct step in regulating emissions of this greenhouse gas.[58] Those rules would require industry to use so-called green completion techniques and more advanced compressors, seals, valves, and other pneumatic equipment, incurring an estimated $530 million per year in incremental industry costs by 2025.[59] Methane only represents about 1–2 percent of US greenhouse gas emissions. But here again, it would be unsurprising were such a regulatory framework to expand in the future to become more stringent or to be applied in some form to existing oil and gas supply infrastructure as well. Any new regulatory costs on the natural gas industry, in particular, would increase unit costs and potentially reduce the number of viable suppliers—marginally driving up the wholesale costs of natural gas and, in turn, natural gas-fired power generation.

And while it is more of a medium- to long-term consideration, a final point worth considering is potential federal climate- or air quality-motivated regulation of the transport and energy sectors that dramatically affects the growth in nationwide electricity demand. As discussed

---

58. Further efforts in progress by the EPA and Interior Department to extend these rules to existing sources, refineries, and federal lands are likely to be abandoned under the Donald Trump administration or overturned under the Congressional Review Act. Enforcement of the May 2016 upstream new source rule could also be deprioritized, or it could be rewritten entirely as it remains subject to lawsuits by sixteen states.

59. In year 2012 dollars, a minor portion of which would be recaptured by the industry in sales of captured gas. EPA estimates that the rule in its current form would increase the price of US natural gas by 0.12 percent and reduce supply by 0.03 percent in 2025 (EPA 2016).

at the outset of this study, one contributing factor to existing nuclear's current struggles in some markets is depressed growth in electricity consumption. There are two main, potentially counterbalancing trends here. On one end is energy efficiency. The Department of Energy has increasingly been involved in setting standards for the energy efficiency performance of electricity-consuming industrial equipment, consumer products, and buildings themselves. Some such efforts enjoy bipartisan support. Current standards cover sixty products, representing 90 percent of residential, 60 percent of commercial, and 30 percent of industrial energy use. New clothes washers, dishwashers, and air conditioners use from 40 to 70 percent less electricity than they did in 1990, according to the US Department of Energy.[60] As federal energy performance standards often follow those employed in California, it is notable that the state has recently strengthened its building codes to require all new residential construction to be "net zero energy" by 2020, and commercial buildings by 2030.[61]

Potentially balancing these increasingly aggressive regulatory efforts around building energy efficiency is a simultaneous regulatory push for increased electrification of both buildings and transport. In buildings, this means replacing the direct end use of natural gas or fuel oil in water and air heaters with electric alternatives. This has not gained significant traction at the national level, but related regulations are under study in states such as California where aggressive emission reduction goals (and mild climates) could be used to justify such efforts.

Another shift could potentially come from the transport sector, where electricity has historically represented only a negligible share of energy use. At least partial electrification of the US on-road vehicle fleet,

60. US Department of Energy, "Saving Energy and Money with Appliance and Equipment Standards in the United States," February 2016.

61. The general definition of a net zero energy building is one where on-site distributed generation (e.g., from a rooftop solar system) roughly equals the amount of energy that building draws from the grid over the course of a year. A net zero energy building can still have significant grid power needs.

or a transition to hydrogen fuel produced from electrolysis (alongside simultaneous decarbonization of the electric grid), would likely be necessary were the United States to deeply decarbonize. Doing so would substantially increase electricity demand from baseline expectations. Returning to the DOE National Lab "Deep Decarbonization" emission reduction study discussed earlier, by 2050 at least 80 percent of light duty vehicle miles travelled in America would be powered by electricity or hydrogen produced from electrolysis, across each of the scenarios modeled—the likelihood of that transformation occurring is far from certain, of course.

From a policy perspective, the federal government has subsidized the electrification of transport in recent years through vehicle manufacturer loan guarantees, a consumer tax credit of up to $7,500 per electric vehicle purchase, and subsidies for electric charging networks. A number of state governments also offer their own electric vehicle tax rebates, charging network subsidies, and even deployment mandates. The California Air Resources Board, for example, operates a zero emission vehicle program which, among other policy support mechanisms, now mandates that manufacturers "offset" 2 percent of their vehicle sales in the state with credits earned from selling full-electric, plug-in electric, or hydrogen fuel cell vehicles.[62] By 2025, the requirement increases to 15.4 percent of sales, by which time the state aims to have 1.5 million zero emission vehicles on the road. The mandate is essentially a cross-subsidy program: credits can be traded among manufacturers, resulting in a current market value of approximately $4,000 per credit;[63] a full electric vehicle sale earns multiple credits based upon battery size. Nine other states have since signed on to California's zero

---

62. The California ZEV Action Plan lists 120 separate action items for various state agencies and organs to take in support of vehicle electrification. See California Governor's Office, "2013 ZEV Action Plan: A Roadmap toward 1.5 Million Zero-Emission Vehicles on California Roadways by 2025," February 2013.

63. Rory Carroll and Alexandria Sage, "California's Zero-emission Vehicle Program is Stuck in Neutral," Reuters, September 1, 2016. This is a decline from an estimated $7,000 per credit value in 2013, when Tesla Motors was estimated to earn $28,000

emission vehicle goals, but achievability of those goals likely depends on significantly better market availability of attractive and affordable zero emission vehicles that match consumer preferences.

Taken together, electrification of transportation alongside electrification in other sectors under a deep decarbonization pathway would result in a doubling of economy-wide electricity demand by 2050, even with dramatic improvements in end-use energy efficiency (Williams et al. 2014).

Congress: Congress could direct federal agencies to use taxpayer money to provide additional sources of income and stability to nuclear owners (or reduce existing subsidies to nuclear's competitors).

Subsidies

The federal government has shown a general willingness across Congresses controlled by both political parties to use taxpayer money to subsidize energy technologies desired by green energy advocates. These subsidies—including tax credits for wind, biomass, geothermal, solar, fuel cell, and cellulosic ethanol technologies; accelerated cost-recovery systems; loan guarantees; and other tax benefits—are described below.[64]

A *wind, biomass, and geothermal power production tax credit* of approximately $24 per megawatt-hour production applies for the first ten years of operation in these facilities. This is the largest federal energy subsidy today. For example, the value of this credit for wind power alone in the United States is currently around $4 billion annually, and it is increasing

---

per Model S vehicle sale in Q1 2013, according to public filings and author calculations.

64. Various frameworks are used to identify and evaluate the magnitude of various federal subsidies to different energy technologies and fuels. See reports periodically issued by the Congressional Budget Office (e.g., CBO 2015) and Congressional Research Service (e.g., Sherlock and Stupak 2015) for the best objective treatment.

alongside the rise in installed capacity of new wind.[65] Today, there is also a smaller production tax credit of about $11 per megawatt-hour for land-fill gas and small hydropower generation. Though it occasionally lapses for short terms, the production tax credit has existed in some form since Congress enacted it in the Energy Policy Act of 1992. It was last extended in December 2015 and is currently set to decline in value before being phased out for new projects by the year 2020. The production tax credit is a major driver of wind power development in particular. New installations have plummeted each time the credit has been allowed to temporarily expire; experts estimate that the credit has been responsible for roughly half of new installations. At times over this policy's history, developers were able to swap this production credit for a onetime investment tax credit of 30 percent of investment costs or cash grants (see below).

A *solar, fuel cell, and small wind investment tax credit* of 30 percent of investment costs applies to both commercial grid-scale and residential systems, as well as a 10 percent investment tax credit for micro-gas turbines, combined heat and power, and geothermal. The 2009 American Recovery and Reinvestment Act Section 1603 grant program allowed renewables developers to temporarily receive up-front cash grants from the government in lieu of the standard investment tax credit (for solar, and also for those periods when wind was eligible for an investment tax credit in place of the standard production tax credit). Originally slated to expire after 2016, the solar power portion of this tax credit was extended by Congress in 2015 through 2019 and will phase out through

---

65. Author calculations based upon state-by-state wind power development and production trends. Distribution of the tax credit is regional in nature due to differences in wind resources and state renewables portfolio standard requirements. Wind producers in Texas, Iowa, and Oklahoma each currently receive more than $300 million in annual tax benefits from the production tax credit. Illinois and Kansas each receive more than $200 million in value. Minnesota, California, Colorado, Washington, North Dakota, Oregon, Michigan, and Indiana each receive more than $100 million annually. Meanwhile, New England and the entire Southeast region each receive less than $50 million annually in their states combined.

2024. Like the production tax credit for wind, the investment tax credit has been a major enabler of solar power deployments that might otherwise be uneconomical.

A five-year *modified accelerated cost-recovery system* (MACRS) for solar, wind, fuel cells, geothermal, and micro-turbines allows tax deductions for these investments to be taken over five years (and about 52 percent of the total cost in the first two years) rather than using a slower straight-line depreciation method.

A *cellulosic ethanol production tax credit* is worth $1.01 per gallon. A previously important corn ethanol blending credit (the Volumetric Ethanol Excise Tax Credit, VEETC) of $0.45 per gallon and import tariff of $0.54 per gallon has expired, as has a biodiesel blending tax credit of $1.00 per gallon.[66]

Project-level loan guarantees fall under a DOE program created through the 2005 Energy Policy Act and substantially expanded in the 2009 American Recovery and Reinvestment Act. They provide federal government guarantees for 50–70 percent of total loans undertaken by qualifying advanced energy projects, with a total authorization level of about $30 billion. In practice, once a project receives a guarantee, that portion of the loan itself is often provided by the US Treasury. Primary beneficiaries have been higher-risk wind and solar manufacturing as well as lower-risk utility-scale renewables generation projects. More recently, federal loan guarantees have been used in power generation carbon capture and storage projects. New nuclear power development is also allocated a portion of guarantees, described below.

---

66. While not a direct government subsidy per se, the Renewable Fuel Standard (RFS), which mandates certain blend levels of biofuels in the nation's overall fuel supply, effectively requires fuel distributors themselves to subsidize biofuel technologies as well. While today's US corn ethanol industry is now efficient and cheap enough that the RFS target is probably not binding (distributors would continue blending corn ethanol at a 10 percent—or even 15 percent, if permitted by the EPA—level without the RFS), biodiesel and "advanced biofuels" (including cellulosic ethanol, landfill natural gas, electricity for electric cars, and some Brazilian sugarcane ethanol) do benefit from this.

Various other subsidies relate to alternative fuel/electric vehicle purchase tax credits, alternative fuel-dispensing station tax credits, electricity in general, thermal power pollution control equipment, advanced technology project loan guarantees, and residential energy efficiency tax credits.

The oil and gas industry also benefits from various *"non-energy" tax benefits:* a "domestic manufacturing" tax deduction (of around 6 percent for oil and gas, which is also available to many other non-energy manufacturing sectors), immediate expensing of intangible drilling costs, accelerated depreciation rates (similar to but generally slightly less attractive than those available to renewables), and reserve depletion provisions (particularly for natural gas and smaller independent producers).[67] Some consider the foreign tax credits used by multinational oil and gas producers (whereby corporate tax credits are claimed for any royalties paid to other countries for production overseas) as a form of subsidy. Meanwhile, oil and gas pipelines, terminals, and storage facilities also benefit from master limited partnership corporate structures that can reduce overall tax liabilities for infrastructure investors. (Recent bills circulated but not passed in Congress attempt to apply these provisions to renewable power infrastructure as well but, surprisingly, not nuclear power infrastructure.)[68]

Overall, the US Congress Joint Committee on Taxation estimates that all of the above tax provisions comprised $20 billion in revenue losses in 2010, rising to $24.2 billion in 2013, before declining to $16.7 billion in 2014. In 2014, 52.8 percent of tax "losses" benefited renewables (including renewable fuels) while 26.8 percent benefited fossil fuels. DOE's Energy Information Administration separately calculated the

---

67. A recent Council on Foreign Relations discussion paper estimates that removing these particular oil and gas industry tax preferences could reduce natural gas drilling activities by 11 percent, increase domestic natural gas prices by 7 to 10 percent, and reduce domestic consumption by 3 to 4 percent (Metcalf 2016).

68. Senator Chris Coons (D-DE) introduced the Master Limited Partnerships Parity Act (S.1656) in the 114th Congress (2015–2016). It would also extend master limited partnership (MLP) status to fossil CCS power generation infrastructure and renewable fuels production and transportation infrastructure.

value of tax subsidies to electricity production specifically at $6 billion in 2013, a figure that rises to $16.1 billion if including both tax expenditures and other subsidies such as direct expenditures, federal R&D, and loan guarantees. Of that $16.1 billion, 72 percent went toward renewables (equivalent to about $22.81 per megawatt-hour of production in 2013), 10 percent toward fossil-fueled generation ($0.61 per megawatt-hour), and 10 percent toward nuclear power ($2.11 per megawatt-hour).[69]

Nuclear power is currently a beneficiary of a few existing federal subsidy programs, many of them stemming from the Energy Policy Act of 2005. For existing nuclear plants, however, today's subsidies are less direct than those available to some other generation technologies. For example, recent changes to the tax deductibility of the money that owners collect from ratepayers and then deposit into plant decommissioning funds, particularly for nuclear owners in deregulated markets (Section 1301), are valued at roughly $1 billion annually. Existing and new plants are also the beneficiaries of a federal backstop to the industry's joint self-insurance model to cover the liability costs of potential nuclear accidents: the Price-Anderson Nuclear Industries Indemnity Act was passed in 1957 and has been periodically extended, most recently to 2025. The act requires that individual plants obtain commercial liability insurance of about $375 million per reactor and furthermore assigns an additional threshold contribution from each US nuclear operator to jointly cover lawsuits arising from the general public which exceed that primary insurance amount, a coverage pool that rises with inflation and was equal to about $13.6 billion as of 2014.[70] For any liability beyond that, the act compels the federal government to make up the shortfall. The act was

---

69. In 2010, EIA estimated the share of subsidies at 55.3 percent for renewables, 15.5 percent for fossil-fueled generation, and 21 percent for nuclear power (the higher share versus 2013 reflecting the value of new construction nuclear loan guarantees). In 2007, the share was just 14.9 percent for renewables, but 48.1 percent for fossil-fueled generation (mostly the costly but largely failed refined coal program), and 18.8 percent for nuclear. See EIA (2008, 2011, 2015).

70. Nuclear Energy Institute, "Price-Anderson Act Provides Effective Liability Insurance at No Cost to the Public," fact sheet, March 2014.

originally adopted as utilities feared that commercially available liability insurance coverage was insufficient to protect against potential future claims.[71] Some regard Price-Anderson as a form of subsidy in that it reduces the overall costs of doing business for the commercial nuclear power sector—estimated by the US Congressional Budget Office (CBO) at a value of about $600,000 per reactor per year (CBO 2008), which is approximately the current average cost of reactor primary liability insurance premiums.[72] Finally, current reactors could be said to benefit from the advanced energy property tax credit, which has been used by nuclear parts and fuel suppliers (but not plant operators) and is worth about $10 million annually.

For new nuclear plants, a federal loan guarantee program was enacted in 2008 with the intent of reducing a new plant's substantial financing costs, which, given capital intensity and long build times, can represent up to one-third of plant construction costs. These loan guarantees were available for 80 percent of a project's total costs, for coverage of up to $18.5 billion in private financing. The guarantees were criticized by some nuclear developers as being impractical given staff regulatory determinations over substantial "credit subsidy fees," reflecting the creditworthiness of the applicant, to be paid up front by developers to the federal government rather than spread out over the life of the project. As of 2015, only $8.3 billion of financing coverage had been taken up by project developers. DOE reworked the program in 2014 to make it more broadly available in hopes of increasing its uptake, including $12.6 billion in capital coverage for categories including fuel enrichment facilities, small modular reactor deployment, and some uprates and upgrades to existing

---

71. The act also covers other aspects of the US nuclear research and fuel chain, both public and private, although public (DOE) facility "joint" coverage is paid for by the US Treasury, not commercial plants.

72. As any actual payouts would require additional federal legislation, Price-Anderson does not otherwise affect annual federal budgets. The oil industry benefits from a similar liability coverage program, the Oil Spill Liability Trust Fund, which does not provide a federal backstop to lawsuits but instead simply limits liability to, for example, $75 million for offshore oil rig operators.

plants.[73] A further $500 million per plant "standby support" guarantee was offered to cover the costs of regulatory-induced delays to new plant construction. The 2005 Energy Policy Act also introduced a production tax credit of $18 per megawatt-hour[74] for only the first eight years of operation for six gigawatts of new nuclear plants, with the stipulation that they be put in service before 2020.[75] Given construction delays of new plants in the Southeast, there have been proposals to extend the service term limitation on this tax credit to avoid stranding about 1.6 gigawatts worth of new construction and to also make it available to the public power entities and electricity cooperatives that are co-owners of some new plants so that they can transfer the value to their for-profit investor-owned utility investment partners.[76]

Finally, the federal government, through DOE labs, research grants, and cost-sharing agreements, continues to fund research and development of new nuclear technologies, including potential civilian power generation technologies such as small modular reactors (Madia, Vine, and Matzie 2015) and advanced nuclear concepts.

In terms of potential new policies, advocates have suggested that some of the federal subsidies described above that are already available to nuclear power's competitors could be granted to nuclear as well. In

---

73. "US DOE will offer $12.6 billion in new nuclear loan guarantees," S&P Global Platts, September 30, 2014.

74. Interestingly, this is the approximate starting level of New York State's proposed Zero Emission Credit nuclear subsidy.

75. This was further capped at $125 million in value per gigawatt per year, slightly reducing the value of this incentive to new plants, given that it would represent a below-average capacity factor of about 80 percent. The total value of this production tax credit, in nominal terms, would therefore be about $6 billion.

76. This is an option currently available to not-for-profit investors in wind power, though they do incur some financial transaction costs in the process of the transfer of the production tax credit's value. See "Resolution 16–09: In Support of Allowing the Advanced Nuclear Production Tax Credit to Spur Public Power Investment in Nuclear Power," sponsored by Utah Associated Municipal Power Systems, MEAG Power, Santee Cooper, and JEA, as adopted June 14, 2016, by the membership of the American Public Power Association at its annual meeting in Phoenix, Arizona.

particular, some have pointed to a production or investment tax credit for existing nuclear as a way to improve the economic viability of the existing fleet. There does not, however, appear to be any precedent for applying such tax credits to existing facilities. A straight production tax credit would be an expensive tool. The current annualized wind production tax credit costs about $4 billion; an equal expenditure distributed over the existing nuclear fleet would fund just a $5 per megawatt-hour credit and would be shared by both profitable and struggling plants.[77]

Applying a more meaningful production tax credit level to just new nuclear plant uprates would be a more reasonable proposition and would be in line with the subsidies available to competing zero carbon energy sources. The nuclear industry has proposed that the current 30 percent investment tax credit for renewables be extended to new investments made within existing nuclear plants, including not just uprates but also spending on refurbishments or safety-related upgrades.[78] Meanwhile, a recently issued DOE expert advisory board draft report has recommended establishment of a direct production subsidy of $15-$27 per megawatt-hour, of an unspecified duration, for any new nuclear power production (DOE 2016a).[79]

Reducing the Impact of Market Volatility

More radically, rather than directly subsidizing commercial nuclear operators, the federal government could use taxpayer money or otherwise exploit its unique low inherent discount rate to reduce the year-to-year

---

77. Author's calculation, as of 2015. PTC cost estimate includes any PTC-equivalent annualized ITC or grant values, if elected.

78. The centrist think tank Third Way estimated that a 30 percent ITC with accelerated depreciation for existing nuclear would reduce plant costs by $3.30 per megawatt-hour when applied to new fuel assemblies alone. Plants undertaking major retrofits could see cost savings of $3.50-$8.20 per megawatt-hour (Robson 2016).

79. This range was recommended based upon the value of avoided emissions from operating a nuclear plant versus average grid emissions in various parts of the country at a social cost of carbon dioxide of $30 per ton. At the top of the range, a one-gigawatt plant would receive about $210 million per year.

Production Tax Credits So Far

The wind PTC may be an effective tool to increase the deployment of wind power and a wind manufacturing supply chain, but it remains an expensive way to reduce carbon dioxide emissions. When the PTC was last allowed to temporarily expire in 2013, US wind installations fell from approximately thirteen gigawatts per year to just one gigawatt. (This dramatic pattern was in part due to a spike in new installations in advance of the anticipated expiry deadline.) New wind installation capacity in recent years has averaged approximately eight to nine gigawatts annually. Without the PTC, Bloomberg New Energy Finance expects that US wind installations would fall to approximately two to four gigawatts annually in the near term, while NREL estimates wind growth without a PTC would be approximately three to five gigawatts annually through 2020.

Regarding cost-effectiveness, a 2013 study of the National Research Council with a team under the economist William Nordhaus analyzed the impact of various federal tax subsidies, across technologies, on overall greenhouse gas emissions (Nordhaus, Merrill, and Beaton 2013). The team found that the wind PTC and solar ITC were estimated to together reduce US emissions by about 0.5 percent, the low figure due in part to the generally small role that renewables currently play in the overall energy system, at a rough cost of $250 per ton of avoided carbon dioxide emissions.

financial risk of operating a nuclear plant. For example, federal public-private partnerships could be established to take on long-term power purchasing agreements from existing (or new) nuclear plants, smoothing out market price volatility over time. This power could then be resold into wholesale markets or pledged to large-scale government customers, such as offices, national labs, or military bases. In many ways, a long-term guaranteed off-take would have an effect akin to a nuclear power feed-in tariff, with the advantage that terms could be more flexibly negotiated to match plant-by-plant situations.

Taking this one step further, were it deemed valuable to rescue particular nuclear plants at risk of closure, the federal government could compel federal power marketing administrations (or other municipal or publicly owned utilities) to take over plant operation from private entities, a sort of voluntary nationalization of assets. These historical entities—including the Bonneville Power Administration, the Western Area Power Administration, the Southeastern Power Administration, and the Southwestern Power Administration (plus the pseudo-independent Tennessee Valley Authority)—already operate and market nearly half of the nation's hydroelectric facilities and four nuclear power plants (the plants themselves are generally owned by the federal government). These nonprofit entities are compelled to sell their electricity cheaply at cost, with the benefit of much of the original capital in aging facilities having already been paid off by the federal government owner. They operate with long time horizons, often with government-subsidized access to debt capital, and are generally regarded as serving social purposes. From a portfolio perspective, therefore, it would not be completely unreasonable for them to take on existing nuclear plants. This would potentially help address the systematic issues whereby privately owned nuclear plants, operating under short-term market-driven investor environments (and if not properly hedged), are under pressure to shutter when unprofitable, even if they might later prove to be profitable in a shifting wholesale market. While the same pressures would apply to any generation technology, one key difference for a nuclear plant is that once closed and decommissioned, it cannot later be brought back online, making the deregulated fleet's continued existence particularly exposed to market volatility.

Carbon Pricing

A broad-based federal price on carbon dioxide emissions—through a carbon tax or a cap-and-trade system—would have widespread impacts on the economic competitiveness of energy technologies throughout the US economy, particularly if paired with a phaseout of major existing government energy regulatory programs or subsidies.[80] While enactment of a carbon price may seem unlikely under the current administration, it would not be impossible if done on a revenue-neutral basis as a part of broader tax reforms, as has been suggested by some congressional and White House representatives. Once opposed by both political parties, a revenue-neutral carbon tax in particular has now gradually gained in bipartisan support if paired with fundamental energy and environmental regulatory reform and rollback. Such an approach has been endorsed by major US firms on account of the greater investment certainty it offers over the status quo; supporters include large electric utilities, such as Exelon and Duke Energy, and even major integrated oil and gas companies, such as ExxonMobil.

In the electricity sector, nuclear would likely benefit from such a policy due to its zero-carbon profile, but also because intermittent renewables might lose relative competitiveness given the added costs to stabilize their output using relatively carbon-intensive single-cycle natural gas peaker plants. Of course, the level of the tax would matter—as discussed above, nuclear power plants today have run into economic challenges and been shuttered even in states with existing, but relatively low-priced (i.e., less than $12 per ton carbon dioxide), carbon markets. A supercritical pulverized coal plant today emits about 1,750 pounds of carbon dioxide and a natural gas combined-cycle plant about 800 pounds of carbon dioxide per megawatt-hour: a $20 per short ton carbon price would therefore increase production cost for the coal plant by around $17.50 per megawatt-hour and for the natural gas plant by about $8 per megawatt-hour.[81]

---

80. What constitutes a "subsidy" in this case would of course be a matter of fierce dispute, but the overall contours are well established, as described above.

81. These additional costs would be relatively straightforward under a carbon tax. Under a cap-and-trade system, actual costs incurred by various generation technologies could vary based upon the use of free permit allocation to existing utilities or generators versus full auctioning.

Another potentially conflating factor for the impact to existing nuclear would be the use of any such revenues generated by a carbon pricing scheme. An economy-wide $20 carbon price, if counting just energy sector emissions, could reach nearly $120 billion annually if collected as a tax (or with full auctioning of cap-and-trade permits). Were those revenues spent by the government on additional socially motivated energy sector subsidies, as opposed to being directly returned to consumers through rebates or other tax breaks in a neutral way, then the end impacts could distort the electricity market and power generation technology development in unexpected ways.

Looking Ahead to Policies for New Nuclear Technologies

While a number of the measures described here could also improve the power market viability of new nuclear technologies once built, the actual development and eventual deployment of new nuclear faces its own gantlet of separate financial and regulatory barriers. Without policy changes, primarily from the federal government, it is unlikely that new nuclear small modular reactors or advanced Gen IV designs will be commercialized midterm.

One aspect is the funding of technology development itself. The DOE currently funds nuclear power research, alongside other energy technologies, through its national lab network (especially Idaho National Lab), research grants to US research universities, and public-private partnerships. This existing bureaucratic infrastructure could absorb additional annual federal research funding to accelerate the domestic development of advanced nuclear technologies. Additional R&D funding could also be put toward better characterizing the safety of existing nuclear plant designs for operation beyond design parameters, specifically reactor longevity beyond sixty-year lifespans (Shultz and Armstrong 2014). In addition to federal funding on nuclear R&D, a diverse ecosystem of private nuclear technology development firms has also gradually built up in recent years: fifty firms across the United States and Canada are estimated to have raised $1.3 billion in private capital toward the development of new nuclear technologies (Brinton 2015).

Streamlining new technology licensing and testing is another potential policy lever. The Nuclear Regulatory Commission (NRC) licenses new nuclear designs through the so-called Part 52 standard design certification process. It has taken steps in recent years to support and prepare for applications from advanced pressurized water reactors, such as SMRs, under a newly formed Division of Advanced Reactors and Rulemaking and its thirty-nine-month, six-phase licensing schedule (Ostendorff and Cubbage 2015). As of 2016, one SMR vendor had announced its intention to pursue NRC review: its design certification application was submitted just before midnight on the last day of the year. But a number of key licensing policy questions for SMRs remain unsettled: reactor staffing standards, security requirements, source terms, emergency planning, and reactor fees.

The agency is less prepared to take on non-light water reactor designs, such as high-temperature gas-cooled pebble bed reactors and sodium advanced fast reactors. The DOE's 2005 Next Generation Nuclear Plant project was established to prepare for the licensing of such advanced prototypes, but here too a number of policy issues remain outstanding. While NRC argues that this situation is the result of diminished nuclear industry interest in actually submitting such designs for review, some investors in new nuclear technologies, especially among smaller nuclear technology start-up firms, point to the lack of regulatory certainty as a significant barrier to technology development. In basic terms, they argue that the NRC should be directed (and funded) so as to more easily accommodate less costly and faster-paced testing, licensing, or deployment of new or experimental nuclear technologies by offering a "test-then-license" pathway. Existing and potential new nuclear-rated component suppliers similarly point to challenges in navigating current NRC certification processes. The lack of regulatory frameworks or expectations for potential "mixed application" SMR uses, such as for large-scale hydrogen production or desalination rather than grid electric power generation, has also been identified as a barrier to innovation and cost reduction (DOE 2016b). The engineering and design of a new nuclear reactor can easily incur $500 million to $1 billion in costs and a decade of time, not including the licensing process. This makes streamlining of licensing and testing all the more important in reducing private investment risks. Here, though, it is important to maintain a balance between the globally recognized gold standard that the NRC licensing and certification process represents and the ability for this system to nimbly accept new technologies under special rules so as to mitigate flight of such designs toward less-rigorous and less-experienced nuclear regulatory and testing regimes overseas.

A third leg of the stool is the need to develop a federal strategy around the construction and multibillion-dollar deployment of first-of-a-kind new nuclear technologies. This is a financing and business model issue (Madia 2015). In principle, the government is not in the business of commercializing new technologies. At the same time, it is very unlikely that a purely private entity will take on the costs of deploying early units of any new nuclear reactor technology even given technology availability from a reactor vendor. This is because there are social costs (and risks) borne by first movers with returns that are unlikely to be captured by one firm alone. Historically, the US government has therefore been closely engaged in the development and deployment of new nuclear reactor technologies—for example, the Navy's development of the early light water reactors as used today—thus helping to drive down their commercial price tags while also directly benefiting from strategic co-benefits such as national security dividends. Concepts for similar options available today include the federal government's direct purchase and deployment of SMRs on military bases or DOE national lab sites (Hamre 2015), establishment of a public-private pooled nuclear technology commercialization corporation along the lines of SEMATECH as used for the rejuvenation of the US semiconductor industry in the 1980s, or the use of federal power agencies to guarantee long-term off-take of new reactor power generation. Any such strategy would likely require up front government financial commitments on the order of $10 billion, with the aim of driving down early unit costs to allow for later organic commercial uptake.

Improving Nuclear's Value

Up to now, we have covered the costs of civilian nuclear power and the ways in which government might choose to improve its viability. But costs could also be balanced by benefits. Nuclear power, as with many other energy technologies, offers two sets of benefits: direct financial value, remunerated through today's energy markets, and external or social values that may be substantive but which nevertheless go uncompensated or are otherwise subsidized outside of the market. What options are available for actually improving both categories of value for existing nuclear plants as a means to improve their viability?

Nuclear Operators: Owners and vendors could pursue plant operations and investments that increase revenues by, or that make nuclear generation more valuable to, the current and future electric grid.

Increasing Uptime
Today's nuclear operators are already generally incentivized to maximize revenues, but nonetheless it is worth looking at additional actions they might be able to take to improve viability. Earlier, we described NEI's efficiency bulletin goals for industry-wide cost reductions and potential challenges. Improving uptime, in terms of the hours a plant generates per year, is another area where the industry has made significant improvements over the past twenty-five years, with average capacity factors climbing from 66 percent in 1990 to over 86 percent in 2012. This was done through fewer forced outages,[82] more efficient maintenance planning

---

82. NRC estimated fleet-wide forced outages at 4.2 percent in 2000, falling to a low of 1.3 percent in 2014, but averaging from approximately 1.5 to 3 percent annually. So-called "fuel failures" include a variety of forms of fuel degradation that can lead to unplanned plant outages or the need for faster refueling. The Institute of Nuclear Power Operations estimates that the rate of annual fuel failures fell from thirty in 2005 to eight in 2012; 92 percent of nuclear units did not experience fuel failures in 2011 (Hawn 2012). Though this was a general

(often to coincide with refueling, despite potentially higher staffing requirements to do so), and refueling shutdowns that are spread further apart and are shorter in duration. NEI reports that the average refueling plant downtime fell from 104 days in 1990 to thirty-seven days in 2001, and it has remained at that approximate level in the years since. The distribution in today's capacity factors, however, suggests that there is still room for improvement at some plants. In 2010, for example, thirteen plants had capacity factors at least one standard deviation below the fleet-wide average.

Today, most plants have adopted either eighteen-month or twenty-four-month refueling cycles, usually carried out during spring and fall low-power-demand periods, and during which one-third of a reactor's fuel rod assemblies are switched out in order to maintain full power generation. This is already an increase from the twelve-month cycles used earlier in the history of the US civilian nuclear fleet. Shifting more plants to twenty-four-month cycles, where feasible, could potentially further increase plant revenues (and reduce replacement power costs, though somewhat balanced by increased fuel costs). More recent proposals envision lengthening this cycle even further—for existing reactors—through a more aggressive fuel reformulation: with minor plant modifications, existing pressurized water reactors are expected to be able to accept fuel assemblies containing up to 40 percent mixed-oxide (MOX) fuels, derived from retired weapons-grade plutonium. The Westinghouse AP1000 Generation III+ reactors, which are currently under construction in South Carolina and Georgia, are potentially capable of running on 100 percent MOX fuel designs. The MOX fuel cycle is more common in Europe and Japan. The US nuclear fleet has little experience with a MOX fuel cycle, and adopting it would rely on operator acceptance, NRC approvals, and completion of a reliable MOX fuel supply chain.[83]

---

improvement in industry performance, it fell below an earlier INPO goal of zero fuel failures by 2010.

83. The US government has been funding construction of a multibillion-dollar MOX fuel fabrication facility in South Carolina in order to meet US-Russian nuclear

Flexible Dispatch

Nuclear proponents often argue that the technology's baseload genera-tion profile (in addition to grid regulation services) helps to stabilize the grid in an era when new generation sources are increasingly intermittent and non-dispatchable. Critics, however, point out that most current US nuclear plants themselves are designed to run continuously, so while they are technically able to be ramped up or shut down on command, they are, practically speaking, "non-dispatched" resources as well. To the extent that natural-gas-like flexible dispatch could become increasingly valuable on power grids with high renewables (or potentially intermittent demand-side resource) deployments, is it possible that existing nuclear plants could adopt such a role?

There are three main issues to consider regarding the US nuclear fleet's ability to "load-follow" by ramping its output over time: technical feasibility, operational feasibility, and economic feasibility.

Nuclear load-following's technical feasibility has in fact been demon-strated in plants similar to those found in the United States—pressurized water reactors and boiling water reactors—according to the Nuclear Energy Agency of the Organisation for Economic Co-operation and Development (OECD) (see NEA [2011] for additional detail). Though specific favored techniques have changed over the years, pressurized water reactors today increase a plant's "maneuverability" by adjusting the mix and composition of control rods or varying the temperature of cool-ant. In typical plant operation, control rods are inserted between a reac-tor's fuel rods to either stop the reaction by absorbing neutrons emitting from fuel rods (fully inserted) or allow full power (fully withdrawn). In certain load-following modes, control rods of varying absorption effi-ciency (so-called "grey banks" and "black banks") are instead selectively inserted into the fuel assembly to more precisely control reactor power.

---

weapon drawdown treaty obligations. While the facility is estimated to be 70 percent completed, its political fate remains uncertain given cost overruns and competing proposals to instead "downblend" and dispose of the weapons plutonium in the New Mexico Waste Isolation Pilot Plant.

This may be accompanied by the use of added boric acid in the reactor coolant loops. Doing so allows a reactor to ramp its output at up to 5 percent per minute (i.e., fifty megawatts for a typical one gigawatt capacity plant) at ranges from 50 to 100 percent of total reactor power. Existing boiling water reactors have more control: because the coolant is boiled directly within the reactor to generate steam, increasing the rate of coolant flow as it is pumped through the reactor core lowers the coolant temperature, densifying it and increasing its ability to moderate the power-producing chain reaction. Existing coolant pumps are able to ramp up boiling water reactor power output at 10 percent per minute (i.e., 100 megawatts for a typical one gigawatt capacity plant) within a range of 60 to 100 percent of rated power output. Lower ramping could potentially be achieved through control rod maneuvers similar to those used in pressurized water reactors.[84]

Reactors in Germany and France (where nuclear has represented a substantial portion of overall generation) have used the above methods for three decades following relatively minor modifications to their existing fleet. Most French plants operate in baseload generation, while some reactors operate in load-following mode, undergoing one or two major load changes each day between approximately 50 and 100 percent of rated power. These daily ramps are generally scheduled in advance, but certain modes allow for a reactor to operate in a low power mode but quickly be recalled to full power on demand. Both would be useful for balancing solar and wind power's output fluctuations, which are both diurnal and minute-to-minute locally. Other plants also participate in primary (two- to thirty-second) and secondary (seconds to minutes) grid frequency regulation, which requires even greater operational flexibility. In France, variable generation generally accounts for 5 to 10 percent of the overall nuclear fleet's output, but can rise to as high as 20 percent on

---

84. More modern Generation III+ advanced boiling water reactors and pressurized water reactors have been designed for regular load-following ability from the beginning, using similar combinations of techniques to those described here, as required by European Utility Requirements (EUR) since 2001. The AP1000 units currently being built in South Carolina and Georgia have designed ramp abilities of 5 percent per minute.

some days. Existing German plants are similarly able to follow load at 2, 5, or 10 percent of output per minute, depending on the total level of load-following desired.

In Canada, CANDU reactors have demonstrated the ability to "dump steam" directly to the plant's condenser or to the atmosphere, bypassing electrical generators and thereby quickly lowering plant output at a rate of about 10 percent per minute down to about 60 percent of normal output. This ramping has been demonstrated in recent years in the Ontario power market, for example, during times of high wind generation at night. Many US reactors could likely do the same, though plant components have not been designed to do so on a regular basis. Only one US commercial reactor does currently adjust its output through "load shaping": Columbia Generating Station in Washington State regularly reduces its output in the spring season when nearby hydropower production is forced to operate at maximum capacity. The boiling water plant can reduce power output to 85 percent with twelve hours' notice from the grid operator by increasing coolant circulation as described above, or to 65 percent with 48 hours' notice by also adjusting control rods. Power adjustments are not currently performed on demand.

Operationally, load-following is a more complex process than continuous baseload generation. Whereas some current industry cost-cutting efforts are aimed at reducing staffing levels, for example, unplanned or even planned control rod or coolant manipulation would likely demand increased plant oversight (though some duties might be handled through automation, regulations permitting). Another potential concern would be the increased wear and tear on plant components given the stress of repeated temperature and steam cycling.

Here, the French and German experience is relatively sanguine: daily load-following has not resulted in noticeable degradation of fuel assemblies or other major reactor component material fatigue, while operational wear components such as valves have required additional maintenance attention. For example, German load-following pressurized water reactors were expected to be able to ramp down to 60 percent of normal output daily for forty years and to 80 percent over 100,000 times (seven times a day for forty years). Newer European Generation III plant designs require similar component fatigue tolerances for daily 5 percent-per-minute ramp rates between 50 percent and full power (20,000 lifetime cycles—see NEA [2011]). Older European plants were also observed to need some degree of additional instrumentation and control upgrades, although this could be less of an issue with the US fleet which has seen a continuous stream of uprates and license extension-related refurbishments. Even so, this might suggest that ramping would be more attractive for plants not expected to apply for extended license extensions of eighty years.

Finally, there is the safety consideration. Would the increased operational complexity of regularly ramping a nuclear power plant increase the chance of an accident? Many nuclear faults or accidents have historically occurred during infrequently performed maintenance or plant testing periods. Beyond a plant-specific technical feasibility assessment, this would certainly be an issue for both NRC and the Institute of Nuclear Power Operations (INPO) to consider and provide guidance on. One obvious approach to reducing related risk might be to concentrate the practice of load-following on a few sets of reactors within a single grid-balancing area so that the practice becomes more normalized and familiar for the workforce within a specific plant.

So the European experience suggests that the existing US nuclear fleet is technically capable of varying degrees of flexible dispatch with relatively minor adjustments. Operational considerations have some uncertainty but could likely be dealt with if desired. But would it make economic sense to do so? At first glance, the case is doubtful. Given the high fixed costs of operating a nuclear power plant and the minimal fuel savings from reducing output,[85] load-following would simply reduce the number of annual generation hours, thereby increasing average generation costs (which, for many US plants, are already too high). In a single load-following plant, annual capacity factors could be expected to fall by about 10 percent. Fleet-wide (or potentially statewide), the impact could

---

85. Fuel costs are about 10 to 15 percent of nuclear plant generation costs, versus about 25 percent in coal-fired and 70 percent in gas-fired power plants.

be moderated, however: load-following is estimated to reduce total nationwide nuclear generation in France, for example, by only 1.2 percent annually (NEA 2011). Therefore, in regulated markets with cost recovery, this level of output reduction would not likely affect nuclear's overall cost-competitiveness versus competing generation technologies. In deregulated markets, however, there is less margin for lost revenue: load-following would either have to follow today's negative price signals or otherwise be compensated through new ISO/RTO market mechanisms or even directed subsidies. If negative nighttime pricing from subsidized wind power is as much of a revenue drain as argued by some of today's nuclear utilities, then the former could be a worthwhile strategy without further policy changes. Otherwise, nuclear proponents would be tasked to argue that better accommodating intermittent renewable power deployment by ramping a zero carbon generation resource such as nuclear has a social value deserving of new policy support. To the extent that increasingly ambitious renewables portfolio standards reduce existing nuclear assets' "addressable market," then such a policy option could be justified, and could potentially mirror the deployment mandates states such as California recently enacted for other zero-carbon grid-stabilizing or load-following resources, such as demand response and grid-scale battery storage.

Pumped Storage

Pumped storage hydropower for grid-scale electricity balancing grew up in the United States through the 1960s, '70s, and '80s alongside the development of civilian nuclear power plants, with a current installed capacity of about twenty-three gigawatts across forty-two plants.[86] Like nuclear power, most pumped storage facilities were developed by regulated, vertically integrated utilities (and rate-based) before the advent of regional transmission organizations. The assets are capital-intensive,

---

86. Data from EIA (2016a). American pumped hydro facilities in 2011 output around 23 terawatt-hours of electricity, corresponding to a "capacity factor" of about 12 percent.

long-lived, site-dependent, relatively slow to build, and heavily regulated. And with the advent of competitive wholesale energy markets, new storage development has been limited in recent years. At the same time, and perhaps echoing the nuclear renaissance era of new plant development heralded during the mid-2000s, new pumped storage applications to FERC have increased markedly, with eighteen gigawatts of new capacity in the approvals pipeline.[87] Despite increased policy interest in promising new energy storage technologies such as batteries and fuel cells, pumped storage (and compressed air energy storage) remains the only economically viable bulk energy storage technology and today represents virtually all power storage in this country and globally.[88] As the US power grid becomes increasingly intermittent and in need of flexible resources, is there an opportunity for a renewed "nuclear-pumped" complementary viability strategy?

Some history is in order. Nuclear power plants in the eastern United States, Japan, France, and southern China have long been paired with large-scale pumped hydro facilities to balance output of large nuclear reactors even without high renewables penetrations: nuclear output at night, when grid demand was low, would be stored in the pumped facility, to be sold back during periods of higher demand during the day. Storage facility generator sets were designed with relatively simple single-speed reversible pump-turbines, which produce power in inclining "blocks" most suitable to the nuclear plant's predictable diurnal variation balancing needs. The value argument for pumped hydro systems in a vertically integrated power system was twofold: (1) they enabled a relatively larger plant to operate on a relatively smaller grid without endangering the stability of the local grid (or otherwise having to attempt more operationally complicated flexible dispatch from the nuclear unit, as described above); and (2), much like a car's hybrid gasoline-electric drive-

---

87. Smith, "Pumped Up: Renewables growth revives old energy-storage method," *Wall Street Journal*, July 22, 2016.

88. Approximately 98–99 percent of storage capacity, depending on the measure used (National Hydropower Association 2012).

train, they increased effective peak daytime output across the paired systems.

Newer pumped hydro facilities in Europe and Asia have, however, begun using or retrofitting more flexible variable-speed turbine and generator sets that are more suited to the minute-to-minute and hour-to-hour fine balancing needs of renewables as well as nuclear. In the United States, CMS Energy Corp.'s decades-old Ludington, Michigan, pumped storage facility has been one of the first to retrofit its generator sets with these variable components, a nearly $1 billion investment. And whereas pumped hydro systems were once the target of environmental activists given their footprint and association with large baseload power plants, they are increasingly seen as a necessary complement to balancing renewables generation without incurring significant carbon dioxide or other local pollutant emissions.

Nuclear owners and operators in the United States could consider how they might invest in new pumped hydro facilities or retrofit existing ones such that they could be operated in ways that better integrate the generation profiles of both nuclear and renewables generation and in doing so maximize the economic value of these fixed assets. The details of such arrangements would likely vary across jurisdictions and markets. In geographically or water-limited areas, this might mean the development of newer "closed loop" reservoir systems. Regulatory support for streamlining the licensing of such arrangements would be a likely prerequisite, as would clarification on the potential treatment of new or retrofitted variable pumped storage facilities as grid (i.e., transmission-type) versus generation-type assets.

Finally, nuclear utilities could take a page from the renewables industry playbook: rely more on long-distance transmission lines to move power from where it is not needed to more profitable demand centers. In the case of renewables, this has meant connecting rural windswept plains or deserts to urban areas. The Texas State Legislature, for example, in 2005 famously elected to socialize the multibillion-dollar cost of new transmission line construction to "competitive renewable energy zones" that new wind power developers could access. For nuclear, could new transmission capacity linking across existing markets provide "virtual" flexibility in power dispatch, shifting demand loads across the network rather than actuating control rods at the source? New transmission lines are expensive and are slow to permit and build, and often face local opposition. But they are also increasingly viewed as a key component of a transforming electric grid that puts a premium on flexibility. Nuclear should be a part of the discussion.

Conclusion

By 2009, applications for the construction of twenty-six new nuclear reactors had been filed with the Nuclear Regulatory Commission. Just five units have since been developed.[89] The failure of the US nuclear renaissance to take hold led observers to ponder the future of civilian nuclear power in this country. Today, the financial challenges faced by existing nuclear plants have led them to ponder the present.

Under a ceiling of low wholesale energy prices driven primarily by the fracking-driven plunge in natural gas prices, nuclear power faces a host of near-term challenges: the deregulated state market and regulatory environment, single-unit plant economics, refurbishment and repairs, slow demand growth, subsidized renewables, antinuclear advocacy, and rising generation costs. A single uniform response is unlikely to be satisfactory: the details of these challenges vary by state and by region. Moreover, not all plants face dire conditions. It is clear, though, from the

---

89. Nuclear's recent development track record (with about 19 percent of proposed projects reaching development or operational stages) has fallen behind even coal-fired power plants, which have faced significant social opposition in the United States on account of their pollution levels. Of the 151 proposed new coal plants identified in May 2007 by the National Energy Technology Laboratory, crowdsourcing anticoal activists estimated that forty-five (or about 30 percent of those announced) were thought to be in development or operation by the end of 2013. "What Happened to the 151 Proposed Coal Plants?" Center for Media and Democracy, http://www.sourcewatch.org/index.php?title=What_happened _to_the_151_proposed_coal_plants%3F.

number of plants which have already shuttered that these challenges are not simply imagined or exaggerated. The reality of the situation is particularly important to understand given that a plant's closure not only means that it suspends generation, but, unlike other power technologies, that the option to return to service in a changing future is lost as well. Plant closures are really two decisions—one short-term, one long—both driven by the market and regulatory zeitgeist of today.

Potential policy responses range from technical tweaks to wholesale markets, to state mandates, to a broad-based reimagining of federal energy technology and development priorities. While there is not a single magical number that would change industry conditions, we do now start to see early examples of policy responses that may be effective, such as the compromise efforts in the states of New York and Illinois. Meanwhile, the federal government has largely remained on the sidelines: will it continue to keep its powder dry, the battle now well-underway? The nuclear industry can take steps to improve its own competitiveness, and it should advocate for the political coverage to do so. In parallel, it is time for policymakers to recognize the values they derive from the existence of this technology in order to make their own case for action. Some values may be very local—the town economy that relies on the existing plant, for example. Others may be far broader—the national competitiveness of future technology supply chains, perhaps. Both matter. Our final nuclear policy recommendation is therefore that jurisdictions across levels make explicit the value that they attach, both in market and external social terms, to keeping the lights on at America's nuclear power plants. Even if local facilities seem to face little threat today, this would make them prepared for if and when existential challenges do arise.

Potential social or other noneconomic values to be considered could include fuel diversity, air pollution, carbon dioxide emissions, cost volatility, fuel security, workforce and communities, supply chains, geopolitical and safety norms, and technology option values. We briefly explore each of these below.

Fuel diversity. What is the value in terms of economic shock risk or energy security to regional portfolio diversity in generation technologies, forms, and fuel supplies? If the benefits are expressed primarily in the "long tail," infrequent but of high impact when experienced, how should that benefit be paid for over time or by different parties?

Air pollution. Strengthening and enforcing EPA air quality regulations such as the Mercury and Air Toxics Standards, Cross-State Air Pollution Rule, and New Source Review have reduced sulfur dioxide and nitrogen oxide pollution in America significantly in recent years. But estimates of mortality from power sector air pollution in the United States are still staggering, ranging from 7,500 deaths annually due to coal-fired power (CATF 2014) to 49,000 deaths annually from the entire power sector (Caiazzo et al. 2013). How should the local and regional human health benefits of nuclear power's lack of air pollution be valued relative to fossil-fuel alternatives?

Carbon dioxide emissions. This study has already discussed the ways in which nuclear might be compensated for its lack of operational carbon dioxide emissions. How can such benefits be considered at the local or state levels (as New York State has proposed), in accordance with local social values, and in the absence of, or in conjunction with, federal action that would recognize nuclear's carbon benefits on an equal basis with renewables?

Cost volatility. Nuclear's month-to-month and year-to-year cost variability is significantly lower than for gas-fired generation and likely lower than for coal-fired generation, while perhaps higher than wind or solar power generation. This translates to changes in the prices paid by electricity end-use customers. While volatility can be hedged (at some cost) through contract terms and financial instruments, there is perhaps additional unrecognized value in the existence of a "natural" hedge based upon the characteristics of the underlying technology. How important is this, and under what circumstances might it become more important?

Fuel security. The cost of preparing for and responding to impacts on basic social services from sudden disruptions such as extreme weather, accident, or attack are often socialized. The severity of costs incurred is also generally concentrated in time or space. This makes it difficult to adequately evaluate the benefit of security through design. In nuclear power, for example, the fuel for many months of operation is stored and available on-site. Coal power plants, by contrast, may have fuel storage of a few weeks, and natural gas plants potentially just a few hours or days. How should this social risk mitigation factor be weighed in guiding investment?

Workforce and communities. Every investment can claim to generate jobs. The NEI claims that nuclear power plants on average employ six hundred people, versus about thirty in natural gas power plants. With their locations in generally isolated communities, nuclear plants can be expected to be an area's largest employer, taxpayer, and philanthropic supporter. (Proposals to close the Diablo Canyon nuclear power plant in San Luis Obispo, California, for example, include $49.5 million in compensation payments to local governments and school districts to partially compensate for lost revenues that have averaged $27 million annually, plus employee severance and $350 million in employee retention costs [PG&E 2016c]). The civilian nuclear industry is also a noted employer of veterans from the US Navy. Are these characteristics socially desirable relative to alternatives? Should plants be compensated in some additional way for that?

Supply chains. Civilian nuclear power plants are the keystone of a nuclear-rated design, construction, component fabrication, and fuel supply chain. Individual components of this supply chain may have nonfinancial local benefits in some areas, while the overall enterprise could have national significance. Does the existence of this supply chain— which also crosses over into the military nuclear power sphere and its own supply chains related to the Navy's one hundred shipboard nuclear power reactors—create value beyond its role in existing markets and local economies? Related is the issue of global competitiveness: Does the United States value a continued global nuclear power technology export role during a period when developing countries' interest in nuclear investment has risen dramatically and even some developed countries may be reinvesting in nuclear infrastructure to meet climate goals? The vast majority of nuclear plants under construction today are now being built by Chinese or Russian suppliers.

Geopolitical and safety norms. Since the advent of President Eisenhower's "atoms for peace" framework, the US civilian nuclear power industry has had indirect relationships with global nuclear rules and norms on nuclear technology development, proliferation, and safety. Nuclear vendors and equipment suppliers operate abroad at domestic safety levels that may exceed the capabilities or choices made by local firms. The NRC established the gold standard for safety, which is aspired to by less-experienced safety regulators. (The NRC even certifies some foreign reactor designs upon request.) Experienced US civilian nuclear employees, managers, and regulators are found in second careers throughout the global nuclear power industry. The most serious nuclear power accidents have occurred outside of the United States. The safety and potential peace dividend of deep US involvement in the global nuclear industry during a time of growth in countries with little to no nuclear experience would be extremely hard to value at the level of a local power plant in the Midwest, for example, but a more dispersed benefit clearly exists at the national or international level. Can such a thing be appropriately valued?

To this point, while we have focused in this study on the United States, nuclear power is in fact under threat in developed countries the world over. Germany, until just a few years ago the world's fifth largest nuclear power generator, has announced a complete shutdown of its fleet; France, ranked third and often held up as the model of a well-run nuclear power system, has announced a cap and drawdown of nuclear's generation share as well. Both decisions were driven by politics. Japan's recovery from a complete fleet shutdown following the 2011 Fukushima accident remains only gradual. The United Kingdom has ambitious plans for new nuclear developments, but the economic future there is fraught as well. In the OECD, only South Korea looks to be a healthy and rising nuclear power—on a stage it shares with Russia and China, and perhaps India. Nuclear power is becoming more the realm of a world beyond direct US influence, as if all at once. This is new and uncharted territory.

Technology option value. As described earlier (box, New Nuclear), promising new nuclear technologies are in development on the horizon, ranging in the near term from the repackaging of essentially mature light water pressurized reactor technology into more advantageous SMR designs, to more extreme Gen IV nuclear breakthroughs, or even fusion power. Some in the general public or political office who may not support today's nuclear technologies and fleet may nonetheless be more optimistic about these new and improved options, especially given global climate change goals. To what extent does our ability to develop the improved nuclear technologies of tomorrow—in terms of education and training capabilities, human capital or simple interest, research facilities, materials availability, and regulatory adroitness—rest on the continued existence of a robust domestic nuclear power industry?

Even for those who may agree that one or more of these attributes have social benefits exceeding current market or policy conditions, it is extremely difficult to quantify them so that they can be considered in an open but nonemotional way alongside the very real alternatives to nuclear power available to us in the power sector today. But complexity should not be a reason to disregard them. As some US states begin to take steps to evaluate potential noneconomic nuclear benefits in accordance with local values, there is a role for the federal government, academia, or even industry associations to play in developing relevant methodologies, frameworks, and analytical tools that could be taken up by future parties to such discussions and used to help elevate that discourse.

Politically, unlike many other forms of energy or power generation, support or critique of nuclear power in this country is not tied to party affiliations.[90] This has often left it without friends when other politically favored energy options have successfully jockeyed for gain. Apart from a few vocal corners and regional pockets of support, Republicans and Democrats in equal opportunity have largely declined to spend political capital on the nuclear sector—something that cannot be said of wind, solar, natural gas, or oil. To take an optimistic reading, this makes nuclear

---

90. A June 2016 Pew Research poll found that 40 percent of liberal Democrats supported expanding nuclear power plants, compared to 37 percent of moderate Democrats, 42 percent of moderate Republicans, and 57 percent of conservative Republicans (Funk and Kennedy 2016). This narrow 17 percentage point spread in support between the two party extremes was exceeded by coal mining (59 percentage point spread between conservative Republicans and liberal Democrats), fracking (52 percentage points), offshore drilling (50 percentage points), and wind power (18 percentage points).

power the rare nonpartisan energy topic, a space shared perhaps only by large hydropower. Amid the pitched battles playing out among energy and environmental advocates across the country, does nuclear power's friend-of-no-one status actually present an opportunity for new coalitions?

As students of the American energy system, we do in the end believe that there is a deal to be made that maintains our nuclear power plants in an affordable and fair way. Domestically, a future we would not want to see is one in which nuclear were rescued from the unintended consequences of existing policy favoritism toward other generation technologies by simply adding another subsidy onto the political Christmas tree. That might well be what it takes to stop the bleeding in the near term—and can therefore be justified as such given the one-way nature of the problem—but those actions should be seen for what they are: Band-Aids. A more lasting approach will require two elements, both of them major political lifts. First, it should have as its target all those nonmarket revenue streams that distort today's energy markets: subsidies, tax breaks, quotas, mandates. Second, in parallel, it should aim to directly reward or penalize not just the immediate financials of market participants, but their external benefits and costs as well—and do so in a transparent way that can be open to further social debate as needed. The most robust and equitable system is one in which the participants would agree to its rules before ever knowing their own eventual place in it. On that count, this ideal, were it ever to be reached, could be embraced not just by those concerned about nuclear power's continuing role, but by any other deserving case, too.

Of course, we may never realize such a utopian framework, and nuclear should not be held hostage to that. In the meantime then, it is incumbent that a floor mechanism be put in place, one which could permit utility plant owners to respond to today's market signals by exiting their nuclear operations if clearly needed, but which would nonetheless preserve the option for each plant to have custodial oversight or be restarted as conditions inevitably change. Existing organs of the federal government are already qualified to take on this new and unprecedented role in response to new and unprecedented risks, but doing so would require leadership.

More broadly, nuclear power's current troubles prompt the larger question of how effectively today's wholesale markets or other governance structures are equipped to manage the clean and high-performance transformation of the US electric grid. Are these institutions capable of delivering long-term strategic goals at a reasonable cost and level of risk, of capturing new innovations and efficiencies, and of incentivizing the participation of diverse players, firms, and business models that will be needed to actually do both? The various policies and programs that were developed to set off the grid's clean transformation in the last decade—defined portfolio standards, targeted production tax credits, etc.—may have been effective in many areas but they are ultimately blunt instruments to rely on to deliver the broader set of social energy priorities going forward. Energy technologies and conditions having predictably evolved faster than governments' ability to react to them, nuclear power's challenges today may be but a canary in the proverbial coal mine.

One final word from Admiral Rickover: In the 1950s, writing indirectly of the schism between futurists and realists, he noted, "Those involved with practical reactors, humbled by their experiences, speak less and worry more." After decades of nuclear operations, we now very much have the experience of what it means, and what it takes, to do so. It is not an elegant promise, but it is a sincere one. And having been split, the atom will not go back together on its own.

Appendix A: US Civilian Nuclear Power Reactors

Plants in Traditionally Regulated States

AL *(27.5% of in-state power generation is from nuclear power)*
    Browns Ferry 1: 1066 MW, opened 1974
    Browns Ferry 2: 1104 MW, opened 1977
    Browns Ferry 3: 1105 MW, opened 1977
    Joseph M Farley 1: 851 MW, opened 1977
    Joseph M Farley 2: 860 MW, opened 1981

AR *(23.5% from nuclear. Grid operators: MISO, SPP)*
    Arkansas Nuclear One unit 1: 842 MW, opened 1974
    Arkansas Nuclear One unit 2: 993 MW, opened 1980

AZ *(28.8% from nuclear. RPS is 15% by 2025)*
    Palo Verde 1: 1311 MW, opened 1986
    Palo Verde 2: 1314 MW, opened 1986
    Palo Verde 3: 1317 MW, opened 1988.

CA *(8.6% from nuclear. RPS is 33% by 2020, 50% by 2030. Grid operator: CAISO)*
    Diablo Canyon 1: 1122 MW, opened 1985
    Diablo Canyon 2: 1118 MW, opened 1986
    San Onofre 2: 1070 MW, opened 1983 *(closed 2013)*
    San Onofre 3: 1080 MW, opened 1984 *(closed 2013)*

FL *(12.1% from nuclear)*
    Crystal River 3: 860 MW, opened 1977 *(closed 2013)*
    St Lucie 1: 839 MW, opened 1976
    St Lucie 2: 839 MW, opened 1983
    Turkey Point 3: 693 MW, opened 1972
    Turkey Point 4: 693 MW, opened 1973

GA *(25.9% from nuclear)*
    Edwin I Hatch 1: 876 MW, opened 1975
    Edwin I Hatch 2: 883 MW, opened 1979

Vogtle 1: 1150 MW, opened 1987
Vogtle 2: 1152 MW, opened 1989
Vogtle 3: under construction
Vogtle 4: under construction

KS *(17.1% from nuclear. RPS is 20% by 2020. Grid operator: SPP)*
Wolf Creek Generating Station: 1160 MW, opened 1985

LA *(16.6% from nuclear. Grid operators: MISO, SPP)*
River Bend: 974 MW, opened 1986
Waterford 3: 1168 MW, opened 1985

MN *(22.4% from nuclear. RPS is 25%–26.5% by 2025. Grid operator: MISO)*
Monticello: 572 MW, opened 1971
Prairie Island 1: 551 MW, opened 1974
Prairie Island 2: 545 MW, opened 1974

MO *(10.5% from nuclear. RPS is 15% by 2021 for IOUs. Grid operators: MISO, SPP)*
Callaway: 1190 MW, opened 1984

MS *(18.5% from nuclear. Grid operator: MISO)*
Grand Gulf: 1251 MW, opened 1985

NC *(31.8% from nuclear. RPS is 12.5% by 2021 for IOUs. Grid operator: PJM)*
Brunswick 1: 938 MW, opened 1977
Brunswick 2: 920 MW, opened 1975
Harris: 900 MW, opened 1987
McGuire 1: 1100 MW, opened 1981
McGuire 2: 1100 MW, opened 1984

NE *(25.5% from nuclear. Grid operator: SPP)*
Cooper: 774 MW, opened 1974
Fort Calhoun: 478 MW, opened 1973

SC (*54% from nuclear. RPS is 2% by 2021*)
    Catawba 1: 1129 MW, opened 1985
    Catawba 2: 1129 MW, opened 1986
    H B Robinson 2: 724 MW, opened 1971
    Oconee 1: 846 MW, opened 1973
    Oconee 2: 846 MW, opened 1974
    Oconee 3: 846 MW, opened 1974
    V C Summer 1: 966 MW, opened 1984
    V C Summer 2: under construction
    V C Summer 3: under construction

TN (*34.5% from nuclear. Grid operator: PJM*)
    Sequoyah 1: 1152 MW, opened 1981
    Sequoyah 2: 1126 MW, opened 1982
    Watts Bar Nuclear Plant 1: 1123 MW, opened 1996
    Watts Bar Nuclear Plant 2: 1150 MW, opened 2016

VA (*39.1% from nuclear. RPS is 12% by 2022 for IOUs, 15% by 2025. Grid operator: PJM*)
    North Anna 1: 903 MW, opened 1978
    North Anna 2: 903 MW, opened 1980
    Surry 1: 799 MW, opened 1972
    Surry 2: 799 MW, opened 1973

WA (*8.2% from nuclear. RPS is 9% by 2016, 15% by 2020*)
    Columbia Generating Station 2: 1131 MW, opened 1984

Plants in Deregulated States

CT (*47.1% of in-state power generation is from nuclear. RPS is 27% by 2020. Grid operator: ISONE*)
    Millstone 2: 869 MW, opened 1975
    Millstone 3: 1233 MW, opened 1986

IA *(7.3% from nuclear. RPS is 105 MW capacity for IOUs. Grid operator: MISO)*
>Duane Arnold Energy Center: 601 MW, opened 1975

IL *(48.4% from nuclear. RPS is 25% by 2025. Grid operators: MISO, PJM)*
>Braidwood Generation Station 1: 1178 MW, opened 1988
>Braidwood Generation Station 2: 1152 MW, opened 1988
>Byron Generating Station 1: 1164 MW, opened 1985
>Byron Generating Station 2: 1136 MW, opened 1987
>Clinton Power Station: 1065 MW, opened 1987
>Dresden Generating Station 2: 867 MW, opened 1970
>Dresden Generating Station 3: 867 MW, opened 1971
>LaSalle Generating Station 1: 1118 MW, opened 1984
>LaSalle Generating Station 2: 1120 MW, opened 1984
>Quad Cities Generating Station 1: 882 MW, opened 1972
>Quad Cities Generating Station 2: 892 MW, opened 1972

MA *(18.5% from nuclear. RPS is 15% by 2020 plus 1% annually. Grid operator: ISONE)*
>Pilgrim Nuclear Power Station: 685 MW, opened 1972 *(to be closed 2019)*

MD *(37.7% from nuclear. RPS is 25% by 2020. Grid operator: PJM)*
>Calvert Cliffs Nuclear Power Plant 1: 855 MW, opened 1975
>Calvert Cliffs Nuclear Power Plant 2: 850 MW, opened 1977

MI *(29.5% from nuclear. RPS is 10% by 2025. Grid operators: MISO, PJM)*
>Donald Cook 1: 1009 MW, opened 1975
>Donald Cook 2: 1060 MW, opened 1978
>Fermi 2: 1106 MW, opened 1988
>Palisades: 778 MW, opened 1972

NH *(51.9% from nuclear. RPS is 24.8% by 2020. Grid operator: ISONE)*
>Seabrook: 1247 MW, opened 1990

NJ *(46.7% from nuclear. RPS is 24.5% by 2020. Grid operator: PJM)*
>Oyster Creek: 615 MW, opened 1969
>PSEG Hope Creek Generating Station: 1161 MW, opened 1986

PSEG Salem Generating Station 1: 1174 MW, opened 1977
PSEG Salem Generating Station 2: 1158 MW, opened 1981

NY (*31.6% from nuclear. RPS is 29% by 2015; 50% by 2030. Grid operator: NYISO*)

Indian Point 2: 1022 MW, opened 1973
Indian Point 3: 1040 MW, opened 1976
James A Fitzpatrick: 855 MW, opened 1976
Nine Mile Point Nuclear Station 1: 621 MW, opened 1969
Nine Mile Point Nuclear Station 2: 1143 MW, opened 1969
R.E. Ginna Nuclear Power Plant: 581 MW, opened 1970

OH (*12.1% from nuclear. RPS is 25% by 2026. Grid operator: PJM*)

Davis Besse: 894 MW, opened 1977
Perry: 1240 MW, opened 1987

PA (*35.5% from nuclear. RPS is 18% by 2021. Grid operator: PJM*)

Beaver Valley 1: 892 MW, opened 1976
Beaver Valley 2: 885 MW, opened 1987
Limerick 1: 1130 MW, opened 1986
Limerick 2: 1134 MW, opened 1990
Peach Bottom 2: 1122 MW, opened 1974
Peach Bottom 3: 1112 MW, opened 1974
PPL Susquehanna 1: 1185 MW, opened 1983
PPL Susquehanna 2: 1190 MW, opened 1985
Three Mile Island: 805 MW, opened 1974

TX (*9% from nuclear. RPS is 10 GW by 2025. Grid operators: ERCOT, MISO, SPP*)

Comanche Peak 1: 1209 MW, opened 1990
Comanche Peak 2: 1158 MW, opened 1993
South Texas Project 1: 1280 MW, opened 1988
South Texas Project 2: 1280 MW, opened 1989

VT (*72.3% from nuclear. RPS is 55% by 2017, 75% by 2032. Grid operator: ISONE*)

Vermont Yankee: 620 MW, opened 1972 (*closed 2014*)

WI (15.5% from nuclear. RPS is 10% by 2015. Grid operator: MISO)
    Kewaunee: 556 MW, opened 1974 (closed 2013)
    Point Beach Nuclear Plant 1: 512 MW, opened 1970
    Point Beach Nuclear Plant 2: 515 MW, opened 1972.

Notes: Summer capacity in net megawatts as of 2009. In-state generation share is for the year 2014. Some plants in regulated states function as competitive facilities and are listed as such. RPS levels are as of mid-2016. Grid operator designations are from Barua et al. 2015.

Appendix B: Recent Nuclear Plant Closures

Closure

    Crystal River 3 (Florida), decommissioning began in 2013
        Reactor had been licensed to 2016.
    Fort Calhoun (Nebraska), 2016
        Reactor had been licensed to 2033.
    Kewaunee (Wisconsin), 2013
        Reactor had been licensed to 2033.
    San Onofre 2 (California), 2013
        Reactor had been licensed to 2022.
    San Onofre 3 (California), 2013
        Reactor had been licensed to 2022.
    Vermont Yankee (Vermont), 2014
        Reactor had been licensed to 2032.

Power Uprate Cancelled

    Cooper (Nebraska), anticipated uprate investment called off in 2013
    LaSalle Generating Station 1 (Illinois), 2013
    LaSalle Generating Station 2 (Illinois), 2013
    Limerick 1 (Pennsylvania), 2013
    Limerick 2 (Pennsylvania), 2013
    Prairie Island 1 (Minnesota), 2012

Announced for Closure

    Clinton Power Station (Illinois), decommissioning announced for 2017
        Originally proposed by utility owner, but near-term closure risk
        averted through adoption of a state subsidy program. The reactor is
        licensed to 2026.
    Diablo Canyon 1 (California), 2024
        Proposed by utility owner through decision not to pursue license
        extension. Licensed to 2024.
    Diablo Canyon 2 (California), 2025
        Proposed by utility owner through decision not to pursue license
        extension. Licensed to 2025.

Indian Point 2 (New York), 2020
Anticipated closure as a result of negotiated state settlement, not averted by state subsidy to other plants. Licensed to 2013 (operating under temporary license).

Indian Point 3 (New York), 2021
Anticipated closure as a result of negotiated state settlement, not averted by state subsidy to other plants. Licensed to 2015 (operating under temporary license).

James A Fitzpatrick (New York), 2017
Proposed by utility owner, but near-term closure risk averted through adoption of a state subsidy program. Licensed to 2034.

Nine Mile Point Nuclear Station 1 (New York), 2017
Proposed by utility owner, but near-term closure risk averted through adoption of a state subsidy program. Licensed to 2029.

Nine Mile Point Nuclear Station 2 (New York), 2017
Proposed by utility owner, but near-term closure risk averted through adoption of a state subsidy program. Licensed to 2046.

Oyster Creek 1 (New Jersey), 2019
Anticipated closure as a result of negotiated state settlement. Licensed to 2029.

Palisades (Michigan), 2018
Proposed by utility owner. Licensed to 2031.

Pilgrim Nuclear Power Station (Massachusetts), 2019
Proposed by utility owner. Licensed to 2032.

Quad Cities Generating Station 1 (Illinois), 2018
Proposed by utility owner, but near-term closure risk averted through adoption of a state subsidy program. Licensed to 2032.

Quad Cities Generating Station 2 (Illinois), 2018
Proposed by utility owner, but near-term closure risk averted through adoption of a state subsidy program. Licensed to 2032.

R. E. Ginna Nuclear Power Plant (New York), 2017
Proposed by utility owner, but near-term closure risk averted through adoption of a state subsidy program. Licensed to 2029.

References

Barbose, Galen. 2016. "US Renewables Portfolio Standards: 2016 Annual Status Report." Lawrence Berkeley National Laboratory (April).

Barua, Rajnish, Miles Keogh, and Daniel Phelan. 2015. "State Approaches to Retention of Nuclear Power Plants." White paper. National Regulatory Research Institute for EISPC (Eastern Interconnection States' Planning Council) and NARUC (National Association of Regulatory Utility Commissioners) (September).

Bechtel. 2014. "Diablo Canyon Nuclear Power Plant Special Studies Final Report: Independent Third-party Final Technologies Assessment for the Alternative Cooling Technologies or Modifications to the Existing Once-Through Cooling System." Prepared for Pacific Gas & Electric and the California State Water Resources Control Board (August).

Bingaman, Jeff, George Shultz, Dan Reicher, Jeremy Carl, Alicia Seiger, David Fedor, Nicole Schuetz, and Ernestine Fu. 2014. "The State Clean Energy Cookbook: A Dozen Recipes for State Action on Energy Efficiency and Renewable Energy." Hoover Institution, Shultz-Stephenson Task Force on Energy Policy.

Bisconti Research. 2014. "National Survey Finds Overwhelming Public Support for Energy Diversity But Awareness Gaps about Energy Sources, Nuclear Energy." Conducted for Nuclear Energy Institute (March 28).

Bisconti Research. 2015. "New Survey Finds Steady Public Attitudes Toward Nuclear Energy, Powerful Impact of Facts about Low-Carbon Energy Sources." Conducted for Nuclear Energy Institute (September 21).

Bollinger, Bryan, and Kenneth Gillingham. 2012. "Peer Effects in the Diffusion of Solar Photovoltaic Panels." *Marketing Science* 31 (August): 900–912.

Borenstein, Severin, and James Bushnell. 2015. "The U.S. Electricity Industry after 20 Years of Restructuring." Energy Institute at Haas working paper (May.)

Brinton, Samuel. 2015. "The Advanced Nuclear Industry." Third Way (June).

Brown, Phillip. 2012. "U.S. Renewable Electricity: How Does Wind Generation Impact Competitive Power Markets?" Congressional Research Service (November).

Caiazzo, Fabio, Akshay Ashok, Ian Waitz, Steve Yim, and Steven Barrett. 2013. "Air pollution and early deaths in the United States. Part I: Quantifying the impact of major sectors in 2005." *Atmospheric Environment* 79 (May): 198–208.

CATF (Clean Air Task Force). 2014. "Death and Disease from Power Plants."

CCST (California Council on Science and Technology). 2011. "California's Energy Future: The View to 2050" (May).

Congressional Budget Office. 2008. "Nuclear Power's Role in Generating Electricity" (May).

Congressional Budget Office. 2015. "Federal Support for the Development, Production, and Use of Fuels and Energy Technologies" (November).

Craig, Paul, Ashok Gadgil, and Jonathan G. Koomey. 2002. "What Can History Teach Us? A Retrospective Examination of Long-Term Energy Forecasts for the United States." *Annual Review of Energy and the Environment* 27 (November): 1–431.

Department of Energy. 2016a. "Secretary of Energy Advisory Board Task Force on the Future of Nuclear Power" (September).

Department of Energy. 2016b. "The Pathway to SMR Commercialization." Workshop, Bethesda, Maryland, June 22–23.

Energy and Environmental Economics. 2014. "Investigating a Higher Renewables Portfolio Standard in California" (January).

Energy Information Administration. 2008. "Federal Financial Interventions and Subsidies in Energy Markets 2007" (April).

Energy Information Administration. 2011. "Direct Federal Financial Interventions and Subsidies in Energy in Fiscal Year 2010" (July).

Energy Information Administration. 2015. "Direct Federal Financial Interventions and Subsidies in Energy in Fiscal Year 2013" (March 12).

Energy Information Administration. 2016a. "Electric Power Annual 2014."

Energy Information Administration. 2016b. "Fort Calhoun becomes fifth U.S. nuclear plant to retire in past five years." *Today in Energy*, October 31.

Energy Information Administration. 2016c. "Annual Energy Outlook 2014."

Energy Information Administration. 2016d. Table 8.1: Nuclear Energy Overview. Monthly Energy Review (September).

Energy Modeling Forum 24. 2014. "The EMF24 Study on US Technology and Climate Policy Strategies." Special issue, *The Energy Journal* 35, no 1.

Environmental Protection Agency. 2013. "Technical Support Document: Technical update of the social cost of carbon for regulatory impact analysis under Executive Order 12866" (May).

Environmental Protection Agency. 2016. "Regulatory Impact Analysis of the Final Oil and Natural Gas Sector: Emission Standards for New, Reconstructed, and Modified Sources" (May).

Federal Energy Regulatory Commission. 2014a. "Staff Analysis of Uplift in RTO and ISO markets" (August).

Federal Energy Regulatory Commission. 2014b. "Price Formation in Organized Wholesale Electricity Markets: Staff Analysis of Shortage Pricing in RTO and ISO Markets" (October).

Federal Energy Regulatory Commission. 2016. "Settlement Intervals and Shortage Pricing in Markets Operated by Regional Transmission Organizations and Independent System Operators" (June 16).

Florida Public Service Commission. 2014. "Review of Florida Power & Light Company's Project Management Internal Controls for Nuclear Plant Uprate and Construction Projects" (June).

Funk, Cary, and Brian Kennedy. 2016. "The Politics of Climate." Pew Research Center (October 4).

Goggin, Michael. 2014. "The facts about wind energy's impacts on electricity markets: Cutting through Exelon's claims about 'negative prices' and 'market distortion.'" American Wind Energy Association (March).

Hamre, John. 2015. "Sustaining American Leadership in the Nuclear Industry." Hoover Institution, Shultz-Stephenson Task Force on Energy Policy, Reinventing Nuclear Power Essay Series.

Hawn, Scott. 2012. "US Fuel Reliability: Improvements and Challenges." Presentation at the IAEA Technical Working Group Meeting on Fuel Performance and Technology (April 24–25).

Herndon, Whitney, and John Larsen. 2016. "Nukes in the Crosshairs Revisited: The Market and Emissions Impacts of Retirements." The Rhodium Group (November 4).

Huntowski, Frank, Aaron Patterson, and Michael Schnitzer. 2012. "Negative Electricity Prices and the Production Tax Credit: Why Wind Producers Can Pay Us to Take Their Power—And Why That is a Bad Thing." The Northbridge Group (September 10).

Illinois Commerce Commission, Illinois Power Agency, Illinois Environmental Protection Agency, and Illinois Department of Commerce and Economic Opportunity. 2015. "Potential Nuclear Power Plant Closings in Illinois: Impacts and Market-based Solutions." Response to the

Illinois General Assembly Concerning House Resolution 1146 (January 5).

Keay, Malcolm. 2016. "Electricity Markets are Broken—Can they be Fixed?" The Oxford Institute for Energy Studies (January).

Krosnick, Jon. 2015. "Global Warming National Poll." Conducted by SSRS for Resources for the Future, *New York Times,* and Stanford University. Topline results (January).

Larsen, John, Whitney Herndon, and Kate Larsen. 2016. "What Happens to Renewable Energy Without the Clean Power Plan?" The Rhodium Group (February 25).

Madia, William. 2015. "The Case for Government Investment in Small Modular Nuclear Reactors." Hoover Institution, Shultz-Stephenson Task Force on Energy Policy, Reinventing Nuclear Power Essay Series.

Madia, William, Gary Vine, and Regis Matzie. 2015. "Small Modular Reactors: A Call for Action." Hoover Institution, Shultz-Stephenson Task Force on Energy Policy, Reinventing Nuclear Power Essay Series.

Metcalf, Gilbert. 2016. "The Impact of Removing Tax Preferences for U.S. Oil and Gas Production." Council on Foreign Relations (August).

National Hydropower Association. 2012. "Challenges and Opportunities for New Pumped Storage Development." White paper.

New York Public Service Commission. 2016. "Staff's Responsive Proposal for Preserving Zero-Emission Attributes" (July 8).

Nordhaus, William, Stephen Merrill, and Paul Beaton, eds. 2013. *Effects of U.S. Tax Policy on Greenhouse Gas Emissions.* Washington, DC: National Academies Press.

Nuclear Energy Agency (Organisation for Economic Co-operation and Development). 2011. "Technical and Economic Aspects of Load Following with Nuclear Power Plants" (June).

Nuclear Energy Institute. 2016. "Summaries of Nuclear Industry Efficiency Bulletins."

Ostendorff, William, and Amy Cubbage. 2015. "Licensing Small Modular Reactors: An Overview of Regulatory and Policy Issues." Hoover Institution, Shultz-Stephenson Task Force on Energy Policy, Reinventing Nuclear Power Essay Series.

Pacific Gas and Electric Company. 2013. "Economic Benefits of Diablo Canyon Power Plant: An Economic Impact Study" (June).

Pacific Gas and Electric Company. 2016a. "Joint Proposal of Pacific Gas and Electric Company, Friends of the Earth, Natural Resources Defense Council, Environment California, International Brotherhood of Electrical Workers Local 1245, Coalition of California Utility Employees, and Alliance for Nuclear Responsibility to Retire Diablo Canyon Nuclear Power Plant at Expiration of the Current Operating Licenses and Replace it with a Portfolio of GHG Free Resources" (June).

Pacific Gas and Electric Company. 2016b. "Retirement of Diablo Canyon Power Plant, Implementation of the Joint Proposal, and Recovery of Associated Costs Through Proposed Ratemaking Mechanisms: Prepared Testimony" (August 11).

Pacific Gas and Electric Company. 2016c. "Application of the Pacific Gas and Electric Company (U 39 E) for the Approval of the Retirement of Diablo Canyon Power Plant, Implementation of the Joint Proposal, and Associated Costs through Proposed Ratemaking Mechanisms." (August 11). Application to the California PUC.

Patterson, Delia, and Harvey Reiter. 2016. "FERC Chasing the Uncatchable." *Public Utilities Fortnightly* (May).

Phillips, Bruce. 2016. "Realizing the Value of Nuclear Energy." Draft discussion paper for the Hoover Institution and Steyer-Taylor Center roundtable on nuclear value and market viability at Stanford University (May).

PJM Interconnection. 2016a. "2019/2020 RPM Base Residual Auction Results."

PJM Interconnection. 2016b. "EPA's Final Clean Power Plan: Compliance Pathways Assessment" (September).

Robson, Amber. 2016. "Preserving America's Clean Energy Foundation." Third Way (December).

Sherlock, Molly, and Jeffrey Stupak. 2015. "Energy Tax Incentives: Measuring Value Across Different Types of Energy Resources." Congressional Research Service (March).

Shultz, Geroge Pratt, and Robert Armstrong. 2014. *Game Changers: Energy on the Move.* Stanford, CA: Hoover Institution Press.

Sweeney, James. 2008. "A Cost-effectiveness Analysis of AB 32 Measures." Precourt Institute for Energy Efficiency, Stanford University.

Sweeney, James. 2016. *Energy Efficiency: Building a Clean, Secure Economy.* Stanford, CA: Hoover Institution Press.

UBS Global Research. 2016. "US Utilities & IPP's Global Research: Getting Nuclear on Nuclear Costs" (April).

Wara, Michael, Danny Cullenward, and Rachel Teitelbaum. 2015. "Peak Electricity and the Clean Power Plan." *The Electricity Journal* 28(4): 18–27.

Williams, James, Benjamin Haley, Fredrich Kahrl, Jack Moore, Andrew Jones, Margaret Torn, and Haewon McJeon. 2014. "Pathways to Deep Decarbonization in the United States." The U.S. report of the Deep Decarbonization Pathways Project of the Sustainable Development Solutions Network and the Institute for Sustainable Development and International Relations. Prepared by Energy and Environmental Economics with Lawrence Berkeley National Laboratory and Pacific Northwest National Laboratory.

About the Authors

Jeremy Carl is a research fellow at the Hoover Institution and director of research for the Shultz-Stephenson Task Force on Energy Policy. His work focuses on energy and environmental policy, with an emphasis on energy security. Before coming to Hoover, Carl was a research fellow at the Program on Energy and Sustainable Development at Stanford and a visiting fellow in resource and development economics at the Energy and Resources Institute in New Delhi, India. His writing and expertise have been featured in the *New York Times, Wall Street Journal, National Review,* and other publications. He holds degrees in history and public policy from Yale and Harvard Universities.

David Fedor is a research analyst on the Hoover Institution's Shultz-Stephenson Task Force on Energy Policy. He has worked in energy and the environment across China, Japan, and the United States. Formerly at the Asia Pacific Energy Research Center and Stanford's Collaboratory for Research on Global Projects, Fedor has also consulted for WWF China, the Asian Development Bank, and the Korea Energy Economics Institute. He holds degrees in earth systems from Stanford University.

George Pratt Shultz is the Thomas W. and Susan B. Ford Distinguished Fellow at the Hoover Institution. He has had a distinguished career in government, in academia, and in the world of business. He is one of two individuals who have held four different federal cabinet posts; he has taught at three of this country's great universities; and for eight years he was president of a major engineering and construction company. Shultz was sworn in on July 16, 1982, as the sixtieth US secretary of state and served until January 20, 1989. In 1989, Shultz was awarded the Medal of Freedom, the nation's highest civilian honor.

Admiral James O. Ellis Jr. is the Annenberg Distinguished Fellow at the Hoover Institution. In 2012 he retired as president and chief executive officer of the Institute of Nuclear Power Operations (INPO). Ellis earlier completed a distinguished thirty-nine-year Navy career as commander of the United States Strategic Command. He earlier commanded the nuclear-powered aircraft carrier USS *Abraham Lincoln*, among other senior shore assignments. A 1969 graduate of the US Naval Academy, Ellis holds a master's degree in aerospace engineering from Georgia Tech, is a graduate of the Navy Test Pilot School and the Navy Fighter Weapons School, and is a member of the National Academy of Engineering.

Index

addressable market, 89
administrative offer price caps, 48
air pollution, 94
Air Resources Board, of California, 68–69
Alabama, 101
American Recovery and Reinvestment Act, 70, 71
American Wind Energy Association, 53
Annual Energy Outlook, of Department of Energy (DOE), 61n52
antinuclear advocacy, 2, 23
antiterrorism capital expenditures, 25
Arizona, 101
Arkansas Nuclear One, 101
atoms for peace, 95–96
auctions, 43–46, 51n41, 55–56, 79n81
availability incentives, 50–52

backup capacity, 37–38
Bade, Gavin, 31n19
base capacity products, 51n41
baseload generation, 6, 12, 26, 39, 56–57, 58
Beaver Valley Nuclear Power Plant, 105
bilateral off-take contracts, 57
biofuel, 71n66
biogas, 39
black banks, 85
Bloomberg New Energy Finance, 77
Bonneville Power Administration, 78
Braidwood Generation Plant, 104
Brown, Jerry, 12
Browns Ferry Nuclear Power Plant, 101
Brunswick Nuclear Power Plant, 102
Byron Generating Station, 51, 104

California, 67, 70n65
    Air Resources Board of, 68–69
    cap-and-trade program in, 42–43
    Clean Water Act and, 59, 59n50
    GHG and, 40n29, 41n31
    low carbon portfolio standard in, 41
    nuclear power plants in, 23, 23n11, 40, 43, 43n37, 59n50, 101, 106, 107
    PG&E in, 18–19, 40n29, 41n31
    RPS in, 19n7, 40n29, 40n30
    ZEV Action Plan in, 68n68
California Council on Science and Technology, 12–13
Callaway Nuclear Power Plant, 102
Calvert Cliffs Nuclear Power Plant, 104
Canada, 81, 87
capacity auctions, 55–56
capacity pricing terms, 50–52
cap-and-trade program, 41n32, 42–43, 78–80, 79n81
carbon capture and storage (CCS), 11–12
carbon dioxide emissions, 4, 10, 60–65, 94
carbon power, zero, 9, 10, 79
carbon pricing, 12, 78–80, 79n81
carbon tax, 41n32, 78–80, 79n81
Catawba Nuclear Power Plant, 103
CBO. See Congressional Budget Office
CCS. See carbon capture and storage
cellulosic ethanol production tax credit, 71
China, 90, 96
civilian reactors, 101–6

Clean Air Act, 58, 60–65, 65n57
Clean Power Initiative Program, 63
Clean Power Plan, 24, 41n32, 60–65,
    60n51, 61n52, 63n54, 64n55
Clean Water Act, 59, 59n50
climate change, 23–25, 97
Clinton Power Station, 41, 41n33,
    104, 107
CMS Energy Corp., 91
coal, 1, 15, 42n35, 58–59, 88n85, 94
    natural gas and, 59n49
    Trump and, 58n48
Columbia Nuclear Generating Sta-
    tion, 43, 87, 103
Comanche Peak Nuclear Power
    Plant, 105
competitive renewable energy zones,
    in Texas, 91
Congress (US), 5, 8
    regulation by, 69–76
Congressional Budget Office (US)
    (CBO), 74
Congressional Review Act, 66n58
Connecticut, 103
Coons, Chris, 72n68
Cooper Nuclear Power Plant, 102,
    106
cost-sharing agreements, 75
Council on Foreign Relations, 72n67
CPV Maryland LLC vs Talen Energy
    Marketing, 33n22
Cross-State Air Pollution Rule, 58,
    94
Crystal River Nuclear Power Plant,
    101, 106

Davis-Besse Nuclear Power Plant,
    31–32, 105
Department of Energy (DOE), 13,
    61n52, 67, 71, 76, 80–82
    National Lab "Deep Decarboniza-
    tion" study by, 68

Price-Anderson Nuclear Industries
    Indemnity Act and, 74n71
depreciation, accelerated, 76n78
deregulation, 14, 15, 16, 31–36,
    103–6
Diablo Canyon Nuclear Power Plant,
    23, 23n11, 40, 43n37, 59n50, 101,
    107
dispatchable generation, 17, 56–57
DOE. See Department of Energy
Dominion Power, 22
Donald Cook Nuclear Power Plant,
    104
Dresden Generating Station, 104
Duane Arnold Energy Center, 14n2,
    104
Duke Energy, 79
dump stream, 87

Earley, Tony, 41n31
Edwin I. Hatch Nuclear Power Plant,
    101
EIA. See Energy Information
    Administration
Eisenhower, Dwight D., 95–96
electric vehicles, 20, 67–68, 72
electricity demand, 19, 19n8, 47–48,
    64n55, 67–68
electricity prices, 2, 15
emission standard, zero, 41, 42–43,
    42n35, 68–69, 75n74
energy and reserves wholesale mar-
    ket, 37–38
energy efficiency, 19, 67
    charge, 56
Energy Information Administration
    (EIA), 13, 14n2, 73n69
Energy Modeling Forum, of Stanford
    University, 12
energy offer prices, FERC and, 47–48
Energy Policy Act, 70, 71, 73–74, 75
energy price caps, 46–49, 46n39

Environmental Protection Agency
(EPA), 4–5, 13, 58–65, 66n59
Clean Power Plan of, 24, 41n32
GHG and, 64, 66, 66n58
ethanol, 71, 71n66
European Pressurized Reactor, 46n39
European Utility Requirements
(EUR), 86n84
Exelon, 16, 22–23, 41, 41n33, 51,
53n44, 79
ExxonMobil, 79

Federal Energy Regulatory Commission (FERC), 4, 8, 32–33, 53,
54, 62
energy offer prices and, 47–48
nuclear power auctions and,
43–46
on pumped storage, 90
uplift charges and, 48–49
Fermi Nuclear Power Plant, 104
firmed energy, 4
FirstEnergy Solutions, 31–32, 31n19
Florida, 30, 101, 106
Fort Calhoun Nuclear Power Plant,
102, 106
fossil fuels, 13, 38, 40n30, 42–43
cap-and-trade program for, 42
carbon dioxide emissions from, 4
MLP for, 72n68
subsidies for, 73n69
See also coal; natural gas
France, 46n39, 87–90
Freeman, John, 23n11
fuel cells, 71, 90
fuel diversity, 93–94
fuel security, 94–95
Fukushima Nuclear Power Plant, 26,
96
fusion power, 96
Future Energy Jobs Bill, in Illinois,
41–42

gas-cooled reactors, 28
Gen III+, 27–28, 84, 86n84
Gen IV, 28, 96
Georgia, 84, 86n84, 101–2
Georgia Power, 30
geothermal, 39, 56, 63, 69, 71
Germany, 25–26, 87, 96
GHG. See greenhouse gas emissions
global warming, 10
Grand Gulf Nuclear Power Plant, 102
greenhouse gas emissions (GHG), 3,
11, 12, 24–25
California and, 40n29, 41n31
EPA and, 64, 66, 66n58
Trump and, 66n58
See also carbon dioxide emissions
grey banks, 85

H B Robinson Nuclear Power Plant,
103
Harris Nuclear Power Plant, 102
hydrogen-powered vehicles, 68
hydropower, 39, 54, 70, 78, 87
GHG and, 24n13
pumped storage and, 89–92

Illinois, 35n27, 41–42, 41n33, 42n35
nuclear power plants in, 51, 104,
106, 107, 108
wind energy tax credits in, 70n65
independent system operators (ISOs),
4, 43–46, 48–58, 89
Indian Point Nuclear Power Plant,
35n26, 105, 108
Indiana, 70n65
INPO. See Nuclear Power Operations
Institute of Nuclear Power Operations, 83n82
integrated resource planning, 29–30
Interagency Working Group, 42n36
intermittent power generation, 5, 37,
52, 55, 56–57, 90

investment tax credit (ITC), 5, 61n52, 76n78, 77
Iowa, 104
ISOs. *See* independent system operators
ITC. *See* investment tax credit

James A. Fitzpatrick Nuclear Power Plant, 35n26, 105, 108
Japan, 25–26, 84, 90, 96
Jobs, Steve, 11
Joint Committee on Taxation, 72–73
Joseph M. Farley Nuclear Power Plant, 101

Kansas, 102
Kewaunee Nuclear Power Plant, 106

landfill gas, 70, 71n66
LaSalle Generating Station, 104, 106
light water reactors, 27–28
Limerick Nuclear Power Plant, 105, 107
load-following, 85–89
loan guarantee programs, 68, 71, 73–75
long-distance transmission lines, 91–92
long-term PPAs, 35–36, 38
Louisiana, 102
low carbon portfolio standard, 39, 41

MACRS. *See* modified accelerated cost-recovery system
marginal cost generation, zero, 55–56
market-clearing price, 14–15, 47, 51n41, 56–57
Maryland, 33, 33n22, 104
Massachusetts, 22, 104, 108
Massachusetts vs. EPA, 60
master limited partnership (MLP), 72n68

McGuire Nuclear Power Plant, 102
Mercury and Air Toxics Standards, 58, 94
methane, 66
Michigan, 70n65, 104, 108
micro-turbines, 71
Midwest Independent System Operator (MISO), 14–15, 50
Millstone Nuclear Power Plant, 103
minimum offer price rule, 53–54
Minnesota, 102, 107
MISO. *See* Midwest Independent System Operator
Mississippi, 29, 102
Missouri, 102
mixed-oxide fuels (MOX), 84, 84n83
MLP. *See* master limited partnership
modified accelerated cost-recovery system (MACRS), 71
molten-salt reactors, 28
monopoly utilities, 29, 44
Monticello Nuclear Power Plant, 102
MOX. *See* mixed-oxide fuels

NARUC. *See* National Association of Regulatory Utility Commissioners
National Ambient Air Quality Standards, 58
National Association of Regulatory Utility Commissioners (NARUC), 14n2
National Lab "Deep Decarbonization" study, by DOE, 68
National Research Council, 77
natural gas, 11, 13, 15, 59n49, 72, 88n85
  auctions for, 51n41
  Clean Power Plan and, 61n52
  methane emissions and, 66, 66n59
  staffing needs for, 45n38

Natural Resources Defense Council, 24
Nebraska, 102, 106
NEI. *See* Nuclear Energy Institute
neighborhood effects, 25n14
net zero energy, 67, 67n61
New England, 15, 51, 54, 70n65
New Hampshire, 104
New Jersey, 51, 104–5, 108
New Source Performance Standards, 60–65
New Source Review, 94
New York, 32–35, 34n23, 34n24, 35n25, 35n26
  nuclear power plants in, 105, 108
  Regional Greenhouse Gas Initiative and, 42–43
  zero emission standard in, 42–43, 75n74
Next Generation Nuclear Plant project, 81
Nine Mile Point Nuclear Station, 35n26, 105, 108
Nordhaus, William, 77
North Anna Nuclear Power Plant, 103
North Carolina, 102
North Dakota, 70n65
NRC. *See* Nuclear Regulatory Commission
Nuclear Energy Agency, of OECD, 85
Nuclear Energy Institute (NEI), 9n1, 15–16
Nuclear Power Operations (INPO), 88
Nuclear Regulatory Commission (NRC), 22–23, 25, 81, 88, 96
  MOX and, 84
  on outages, 83n82, 84
nuclear rescue bill, in Illinois, 35n27

Obama, Barack, 11, 13, 24, 60–65, 60n51, 66
Oconee Nuclear Power Plant, 103
OECD. *See* Organisation for Economic Co-operation and Development
Ohio, 31–32, 31n19, 39n28, 105
oil, 72
Oil Spill Liability Trust Fund, 74n71
Oregon, 70n65
Organisation for Economic Co-operation and Development (OECD), 85
outages, 83–84, 83n82
overcapacity, 15
Oyster Creek Nuclear Power Plant, 51, 104, 108

Pacific Gas and Electric (PG&E), 18–19, 40n29, 41n31
Palisades Nuclear Power Plant, 104, 108
Palo Verde Nuclear Power Plant, 101
Part 52 standard certification process, of NRC, 81
Pathways to Deep Carbonization, 11–12
Peach Bottom Nuclear Power Plant, 22–23, 105
pebble bed reactors, 28
peer effects, 25n14
Pennsylvania, 22–23, 51, 105, 107
Perry Nuclear Power Plant, 105
PG&E. *See* Pacific Gas and Electric
Pilgrim Nuclear Power Station, 22, 104, 108
PJM Interconnection, 14, 15, 31–32, 50–54, 51n41, 63
Point Beach Nuclear Plant, 14n2, 106
policymakers, recommendations for, 7–9
politics, 97–98, 97n90

positive externalities, 6
power purchase agreements (PPAs),
    31–33, 31n19, 35–36, 38
PPL Susquehanna Nuclear Power
    Plant, 105
Prairie Island Nuclear Power Plant,
    102, 107
Price-Anderson Nuclear Industries
    Indemnity Act, 73–74, 74n71
production tax credit (PTC), 4, 5, 54
    for wind energy, 15, 53, 53n43,
    53n45, 61n52, 77
project-level loan guarantees, 71
prudence review, 29
PSEG Hope Creek Generating Sta-
    tion, 104
PSEG Salem Generating Station, 105
PTC. See production tax credit
public goods charge, 56
public utility commissions (PUCs),
    3–4, 28–29
public-private partnerships, 77
PUCs. See public utility commissions
pumped storage, 89–92, 89n86

Quad Cities Nuclear Power Plant, 41,
    41n33, 51, 53n44, 104, 108

R. E. Ginna Nuclear Power Plant,
    35n26, 105, 108
ratcheting, in RPS, 65, 65n56
rate cases, 30
R&D. See research and development
refueling cycles, 18, 47, 83n82, 84
Regional Greenhouse Gas Initiative,
    in California, 42–43
regional transmission organizations
    (RTOs), 4, 48–49, 89
    auctions by, 43–46, 55–56
    availability incentives by, 50–51
    energy market price setting by,
    52–58

regulation
    with availability incentives, 50–52
    with capacity pricing terms, 50–52
    by Congress, 69–76
    with energy price caps, 46–49
    increasing costs of fossil fuel power
    generation, 42–43
    nuclear generation mandates,
    39–42
    options for, 28–82
    for R&D, 80–81
    reducing renewables cost to cus-
    tomers, 36–38
    by states, 28–30, 101–3
    transactive pricing framework,
    57–58
    with uplift charges, 48–49
    zero emission standard, 68–69
    See also specific federal agencies,
    acts, and programs
renewable energy, 8, 10, 11, 36–38,
    52–58
    in California, 18–19
    Clean Power Plan and, 62–63
    long-term PPAs for, 38
    solar, 18, 39, 52, 61n52, 71, 77
    subsidies for, 4, 10, 37–38, 54,
    54n46, 69–76, 73n69
    tax credits for, 52–53, 54
    See also hydropower; wind energy
Renewable Fuel Standard (RFS),
    71n66
renewables portfolio standards (RPS),
    18, 39–40, 39n28, 41, 56
    in California, 19n7, 40n29, 40n30
    PG&E and, 40n29
    ratcheting in, 65, 65n56
research and development (R&D),
    80–81
reserves payments, 37
revenue-neutral carbon tax, 5, 6
RFS. See Renewable Fuel Standard

Rhodium Group, 13, 61n52
Rickover, Hyman, 7, 99
River Bend Nuclear Power Plant, 102
RPS. *See* renewables portfolio
    standards
RTOs. *See* regional transmission
    organizations
Russia, 96

safety, 3, 22, 26, 45n38, 88, 95–96
San Onofre Nuclear Generating Sta-
    tion, 43, 101, 106
Seabrook Nuclear Power Plant, 104
SEMATECH, 82
Sequoyah Nuclear Power Plant, 103
shale gas, 15
short-run marginal cost of operation,
    47
short-term cost minimization, 6
Sierra Club, 24
single-unit sites, 17, 22
small modular nuclear reactors
    (SMRs), 18, 81–82, 96
solar, fuel cell, and small wind invest-
    ment tax credit, 70–71
solar energy, 18, 39, 52, 61n52, 71, 77
South Carolina, 30, 84, 84n83,
    86n84, 103
South Korea, 96
South Text Project, 105
Southeast, 19n8, 70n65, 75
Southeastern Power Administration,
    78
Southern California Edison, 22
Southwestern Power Administration,
    78
St. Lucie Nuclear Power Plant, 101
Stanford University, 12
states
    with antinuclear advocacy, 23
    Clean Air Act and, 65n57
    deregulation in, 14, 31–33, 103–6

legislative action in, 4
nuclear power mandates in, 38–42
PUCs in, 3–4, 28–29
regulation by, 28–30, 101–3
stationary-source regulations, for
    GHG, 64
strategic reserve, 17n5
subsidies, 34n24, 54
    for electric vehicles, 20, 72
    for nuclear power, 10, 73–74, 73n69
    for renewable energy, 4, 10, 37–38,
        54, 54n46, 69–76, 73n69
    See also tax credits
supply chains, 95
Surry Nuclear Power Plant, 103

tax credits, 72, 75
    ITC, 5, 61n52, 76n78, 77
    for renewable energy, 52–53, 54
    wind, biomass, and geothermal
        power production, 69–70
    for wind energy, 69–70, 70n65
    See also production tax credit
Tennessee, 103
Texas, 26, 91, 105
Third Way, 76n78
Three Mile Island Nuclear Power
    Plant, 51, 105
Toshiba-Westinghouse AP1000, 27,
    84, 86n84
transactive pricing framework,
    57–58
Trump, Donald, 11, 58n48, 60n51, 64,
    66n58
Turkey Point Nuclear Power Plant,
    101

uplift charges, 48–49
uptime, 83–84, 83n82

V C Summer Nuclear Power Plant,
    103

VEETC. *See* Volumetric Ethanol Excise Tax Credit
vehicles
electric, 20, 67–68, 72
zero emission standard for, 68–69
Vermont Yankee Nuclear Power Plant, 105, 106
very-high-temperature reactors, 28
Virginia, 22, 103
Vogtle Nuclear Power Plant, 102
volumetric energy commodity charge, 34n23
Volumetric Ethanol Excise Tax Credit (VEETC), 71

Wara, Michael, 64n55
Washington, 29, 43, 70n65, 87, 103
Waterford Nuclear Power Plant, 102
Watts Bar Nuclear Plant, 103

Western Area Power Administration, 78
wind, biomass, and geothermal power production tax credit, 69–70
wind energy, 13, 52, 53n44, 71
PTC for, 15, 53, 53n43, 53n45, 61n52, 77
tax credits for, 69–70, 70n65
Wisconsin, 106
Wolf Creek Generation Station, 102
workforce, 95

zero carbon power, 9, 10, 79
zero emission standard, 41, 42–43, 42n35, 68–69, 75n74
zero marginal cost generation, 55–56
ZEV Action Plan, in California, 68n68

SHULTZ-STEPHENSON TASK FORCE ON

Energy Policy

The Hoover Institution's Shultz-Stephenson Task Force on Energy Policy addresses energy policy in the United States and its effects on our domestic and international political priorities, particularly our national security.

As a result of volatile and rising energy prices and increasing global concern about climate change, two related and compelling issues—threats to national security and adverse effects of energy usage on global climate—have emerged as key adjuncts to America's energy policy; the task force will explore these subjects in detail. The task force's goals are to gather comprehensive information on current scientific and technological developments, survey the contingent policy actions, and offer a range of prescriptive policies to address our varied energy challenges. The task force will focus on public policy at all levels, from individual to global. It will then recommend policy initiatives, large and small, that can be undertaken to the advantage of both private enterprises and governments acting individually and in concert.

Contact for the Shultz-Stephenson
Task Force on Energy Policy:
Jeremy Carl, *Research Fellow*
(650) 723-2136
carljc@stanford.edu

About the Reinventing Nuclear Power Series

The energy landscape in the United States has been reshaped since the development of our commercial nuclear power fleet. Innovations in horizontal drilling and hydraulic fracturing of shale source rock have made this country "the Saudi Arabia of natural gas" by reimagining the production of resources once thought unexploitable. Wind and solar power dot the landscape, driven by supporting policy but also by continuous advances in technological performance, manufacturing, and business strategy. They have evolved from science experiments to now justifying their own roles on our changing electric grids. Meanwhile, rethinking how we use our energy, from LED lighting to low-heat-loss windows, has dramatically improved efficiency and disrupted the curve on electricity demand. Over the past decades, nuclear power has been an affordable, reliable, and low-polluting pillar of our energy system; as we look to the future, can it too be reinvented to sustain and enhance the nuclear contribution in a newly diverse and robust energy industrial landscape?

Our purpose in the Shultz-Stephenson Task Force on Energy Policy's Reinventing Nuclear Power project is to offer a technically grounded and policy-informed assessment of the case for a US civilian nuclear future in a modernizing grid. To do this, we have asked experts from around the country to use a fresh mind to identify the largest obstacles to shaping national energy policies in this area and the decision points around them, to specify potential roles for government, military, and the private sector, and, finally, to propose solutions in defining a way forward.

As Exelon Corporation's John Rowe once noted, "Nuclear is a business, not a religion." And unlike articles of faith, the market requires constant reinvention to stay relevant. Ultimately, objective merits should determine how and if nuclear power is able to fulfill its full promise. US leadership in developing and fostering a global civilian nuclear power ecosystem over the past half-century is undeniable. In this new energy landscape, it is our hope that the American nuclear enterprise can build on this precedent to legitimately reinvent itself for the next.

—George P. Shultz and James O. Ellis Jr.